Despite decades of research describing transferring from a two-year to a fou has been made in helping more of them succeed. By paying keen attention to the voices of these students and the stories they tell – such as
those summarized in this book – fresh policy and practice alternatives
may emerge that can help them and their schools effectively manage this
challenging transition.*
~ George D. Kuh, Chancellor's Professor of Higher Education
Emeritus, Indiana University

*Through the narratives of these Latina students starting out in two-year
colleges, the book focuses on four major facets that helped shape their experiences and ultimately their life choices: an inner, heartfelt emotional
and psychological support from significant others; support for establish-
ing goals and choosing a career path; support targeted at advancing a
student's knowledge pertinent to their particular field of study; and finding influential role models. These four domains are interwoven in their
interactions and relationships with family, faculty, peers, and academic
staff. Much of what is revealed in these stories may provide new and
fresh perspectives on how to help students deal successfully with the
challenges in transferring.* ~ Amaury Nora, Professor, Associate
Dean for Research, & Director, Center for Research and Policy in
Education, University of Texas at San Antonio

*The research published on Latino student success rarely focuses on the
narrative from the Chicana/Latina perspective. Dr. Espinoza brings to
light the critical issues and hurdles that impact Latina students in the
community college system. This text provides the research and stories
that educational practitioners need in order to implement new policies,
practices, and strategies that will create successful transfer pathways
for Latinas. It is an inspirational text that provides intimate details of
the aspirational capital that colleges need to support and develop for
women of color.* ~ Miguel A. Alvarez, Assistant Director, Undergraduate Admissions, University of California, Berkeley

It was my privilege to serve on the dissertation committee of Dr. Lily E. Espinoza. Her research into the lived experience of Latina transfer students provided a new dimension of understanding the obstacles students face in their educational journey. The student narratives showcased success strategies that helped them reach their goals and which can be applied by educators. I am thrilled that these student voices and experiences will now reach a wider audience. ~ John C. Hernandez, Interim President, Santiago Canyon College, Orange, California

Higher education has done a better job as of late in tracking Latino/a/x students from high school through community colleges and on to four-year colleges and universities, but largely missing from this unique pathway in higher education are the stories of students for whom this is their lived experience. This valuable book begins to fill that gap, and it does so in powerful ways. ~ John Hoffman, Associate Professor and Chair School of Education, California State University, Fullerton

Not Getting Stuck

Not Getting Stuck

Success stories of being Latina
and transferring from a California community college

Lily E. Espinoza

Alive Book Publishing

Not Getting Stuck
Copyright © 2017 by Lily E. Espinoza

Additional copies may be ordered from the publisher for educational, business, promotional or premium use.
For information, contact ALIVE Book Publishing at:
alivebookpublishing.com, or call (925) 837-7303.

Book Design by Alex Johnson
Cover art: Cecilia Méndez, *linaje/lineage (lines)*, ink on paper, ©2003.
Photograph by Frank Graham

ISBN 13
978-1-63132-039-2

ISBN 10
1-63132-039-4

Library of Congress Control Number: 2017939472

Library of Congress Cataloging-in-Publication Data
is available upon request.

First Edition

Published in the United States of America by ALIVE Book Publishing
and ALIVE Publishing Group, imprints of Advanced Publishing LLC
3200 A Danville Blvd., Suite 204, Alamo, California 94507
alivebookpublishing.com

PRINTED IN THE UNITED STATES OF AMERICA

10 9 8 7 6 5 4 3 2 1

For my family, especially my son, Justice

Table of Contents

Don't Quit

When things go wrong, as they sometimes will,
When the road you're trudging seems all uphill,
When funds are low and the debts are high,
And you want to smile but you have to sigh,
When care is pressing you down a bit,
Rest if you must, but don't you quit.

Life is queer with its twists and turns,
As every one of us sometimes learns,
And many a failure turns about,
When he might have won if he'd stuck it out.
Don't give up, though the pace seems slow -
You may succeed with another blow.

Often the goal is nearer than
It seems to a faint and faltering man;
Often the struggler has given up
When he might have captured the victor's cup,
And he learned too late, when the night slipped down,
How close he was to the golden crown.

Success is failure turned inside out -
The silver tint of the clouds of doubt,
And you never can tell how close you are -
It may be near when it seems afar;
So stick to the fight when you're hardest hit -
It's when things seem worst that you mustn't quit.

—Anonymous

Foreword

"Something's gotta give," I told myself, before opening the door of the Fullerton College Transfer Center. I was convinced that I was going to make it happen; I was going to transfer. Too much time had passed and I was still at Fullerton College. I knew I needed to transfer to a university the following fall semester. However, the leap from a community college to a university felt like an arduous task. Thus, similar to the many voices in this anthology, I needed someone's guidance and expertise. Once the door to the Transfer Center closed behind me, I met Dr. Lily Espinoza who was the director of the transfer center, and the person who would guide me. In fact, little did I know but Dr. Espinoza would become more than just the person who would help me transfer; she would become my friend and confidante. Dr. Espinoza is a prime example of a strong, courageous Latina who made it! She shattered the glass ceiling of the educational world. As a doctoral recipient, she made her way, getting her doctorate, her Master's and Bachelor's Degrees via the finest academic institutions including the Ivy League. As I write this foreword, her story fills me with such inspiration! I can only imagine the countless others she inspired with her story. A story that could be yours as well! Because we are all searching to better ourselves, our families, and our communities.

It is important for me to emphasize that meeting Lily changed my life. I had been at Fullerton College for two years.

I didn't want to admit it, but I was feeling stuck, stuck in time and in space. I went into the center hoping to meet someone who could answer my questions and help me feel at ease. I visited the Transfer Center the previous year, but I felt turned off. What helped me bridge the gap between myself and the Transfer Center was my mantra, "I'm just one person. I want to transfer. This is the place that will help me achieve my goal." I particularly remember Dr. Espinoza's door was always open, and she never turned me away. Dahlia, one of the voices in this anthology, says it best when she describes meeting her counselor Joe Reyes and her EOPS support system, "It was almost like a gift".

When I was reading *Not Getting Stuck*, I saw my own transfer journey exemplified in the nine narratives presented here. I, too, am Latina. I transferred to U.C. Berkeley, just as Lily did. These stories reflect many of the same struggles that I experienced during the transfer process. It was eye-opening for me to see that so many other Latina women and I shared similar experiences. I remember feeling, at times, engulfed by the stress and the burden of school and family, deadlines and the pressure to transfer quickly. Unfortunately, it is not difficult to see why so many community college students do not transfer to a university. It is so easy to put off the process for another year. As Sapphire explains in the chapter *Breaking Stereotypes*, "I had this impression that once you get here, you get sucked in and you can't get out...I'm here. I'm going to transfer. I'm not going to get stuck". This is why a book like *Not Getting Stuck* is sorely needed. Through the personal narratives of the women featured in it, one finds that they are not alone, and that others have overcome similar adversities in order to transfer to a university.

Additionally, these narratives provide a window into the hardest aspects of the transfer process; some of them personal and some bureaucratic. When you're living through it, transferring seems like a herculean challenge. However, once you get yourself through the hardships, you can succeed at the university! Transferring involves strife, so when one manages to succeed, you see that anything is possible. You become more secure with yourself and your self-confidence increases. As Bellaise, one of the ladies in the book recounts, "[the transfer journey] helped me mentally believe in myself more...I got a lot stronger and a lot surer of myself". Similarly, Paula's recalls, "When I did transfer, it made me feel like, see I can do it. I felt like I can achieve something...I did it. It was really exciting for me". It cannot get more empowering than that!

"Life begins at the end of your comfort zone," perfectly summed it up by Neal Donald Walsch. Exactly one year after my first attempt to seek help in the transfer process, I recall the feeling of shame and guilt for not having transferred the year before. My first experience at the Transfer Center was uncomfortable, because I had no connection with the counselor who was helping me. The counselor was a white male; he didn't share my story nor my identity or struggles; his vibe and condescending tone turned me off. However, a person cannot let one negative experience stop them. Thus, one needs to seek out a connection with someone who can help. Someone who will help them feel like they are not alone on their journey. As Paula suggests, "I would recommend students talk to counselors but not just anybody. Try to find a counselor who can go there with you. Not just to talk about transferring but somebody that can just talk". It is essential to find someone who sees your potential, like Joe saw in Dahlia: "He saw what I didn't see...that was so nurturing for me. He fed my spirit and helped me to keep moving toward my goal...he helped build that inside of myself". Additionally, once you are able to actualize your potential, you can begin to do amazing things. For instance, Dahlia had a sort of epiphany through the help of her mentor who helped her to see her potential, "that's what the support helped me to do. It helped me see myself, as a person that was shaping my own life". As we see in her story, he propels her to apply to one of the finest schools in the UC system, where she is accepted.

A support system is central to one's success in community college, but ultimately as you will see in all nine of the narratives—it is self-determination that matters the most. If you don't want it for yourself, if you don't motivate yourself, then you're not going to go anywhere. It comes down to your own drive in the end because you're the one who must attend all the lectures, office hours, study groups, take the exams, and write term paper after term paper. You must walk yourself across the street to meet with the counselors; you must sign yourself up for transfer workshops; you must go on college tours; you must fight for a spot in a class; you are at the center of everything. You must be a warrior! You must also give yourself credit. After all, everything you do, you ultimately do by yourself. Dana makes this resonate in her final remarks, "I hope other Latinas realize, do it for your family and do it for everyone else in your community, but most importantly, do it for you. You deserve it. You don't have to feel guilty for leaving everyone else behind". Yes, your family is important. Yes, your community is important, but you have to want to do it for yourself first.

Often times, as you will read in these first-hand accounts, family is at the core of the transfer decision. Several ladies voiced that they wanted to stay relatively close to home, as if they couldn't see themselves going far away, one even commuted from home three, even four hours a day on the bus to UCLA to stay with her family. This is a question we all face, "Do I stay or do I go? Can I leave my family behind?" The answer is, "Yes, yes you can!" Don't feel guilty.

As a Latina transfer student, reading through each personal narrative, it brought back so many emotions. Dr. Espinoza highlights the importance of realizing you're not alone on the long, winding road to transfer and how you should never allow your-self to settle for less than the best. As Sapphire perfectly stated, "I don't have to limit myself. I can go anywhere". Just like these nine inspiring women presented in this book, there are and have been others that have taken on the challenge and won. They re-alized how important it is to draw inspiration and guidance from somewhere and someone. It is too easy at first glance to miss the success stories because you do not see too many out there, but once you search for them, you will find them. And then you too can go back into your own community and inspire others as you were inspired!

When I finished reading *Not Getting Stuck*, I thought "Wow! If only I had read something like this when I was in community college!" Especially during those moments when I felt alone, scared, discouraged and melancholic about the transfer process. Reading and knowing about others succeeding, while you are struggling is motivating. In Sapphire's section she tells the read-ers that "A good student support program should have not only peer mentors but professional mentors. Latina women who have lived the experience and have come out on the other side as very successful". We're all in the same boat and we need to hear that, as well as having someone who can propel us to succeed, to achieve our goals and dreams. This book is inspiring! It pro-vides real accounts from Latina women who faced hardships and made it through.

Additionally, this book takes the reader through the com-munity college-university trajectory. It includes information about where they are now and how far they have come. I couldn't agree more with one of Sapphire's concluding remarks "Latinas in community college need to see that it's possible". Yes, they do and now with this book, many Latina women will see for themselves. This book is perfect literature for a career planning or a general counseling class, because when you don't know exactly what classes to take or what major to declare, that is when you struggle the most with your self-doubt. Reading a book like *Not Getting Stuck* can make the difference for anyone thinking they can't get out of that time-space continuum we call the community college. *Si se puede!*

Melissa Zazueta
Fullerton College, 2011
University of California, Berkeley
B.A. History, 2014

Preface

Rare it is to hear the voices of Latina transfer students included in discussions around access, opportunity and achievement in higher education policy development. Far too often quantitative factors alone are used as the backdrop for research that influences higher education enrollment management, workforce development, degree attainment, college preparation, marketing, recruitment, and K-16 partnerships. Rarer is it to see the inclusion of life stories, memories, reflections, relationships, recollections, thoughts, impressions, perceptions, cultural references, lived experiences, and emotions of those affected most by these policies.

This anthology brings forth the voices of Latina students at a California community college to serve as a platform for discussion on how to improve college degree attainment for all. These stories represent shared experiences that many students face as they take the first step on the road to pursuing a college education. As well, these stories represent some of the hidden factors that must be included in the discourse on improving the educational pipeline in the United States.

The impetus for this work began with the research I conducted for my dissertation in Educational Leadership with a focus on Community College Leadership. As a Latina community college transfer student I was curious to hear and learn from others about their transfer experience. I wanted to study what it was like for others who transferred out of a community college.

As a graduate student attending an Ivy League institution, I recalled the sensation of being looked upon as if I was a purple unicorn because I somehow managed to make it out of a community college and transfer to a university. Not only did I transfer, but I was pursuing a graduate degree. Was I really that much of an anomaly? In scouring the educational research on community college transfer student success, I learned the dismal reality. The majority of community college students, not to mention Latina students in particular, far more often than not, fail to transfer and fail to complete their baccalaureate education. The knowledge I gained in my master's level graduate work intensified my curiosity to seek out more information about the experience of others who successfully crossed the border, so to speak, from the community college to the hallowed halls of the university. This curiosity manifested itself in my dissertation, which was aimed at providing data to influence higher education policy at the local, state, and federal level.

In my dissertation study, I conducted two focus group interviews in addition to nine individual interviews. In total, I interviewed 20 successful Latina transfer students from the same California community college. I developed the Transfer Student College Choice Model as a result of interpreting over 150 meaning units from the interviews. I identified six themes that impacted college choice and provided recommendations for further research and practice in higher education administration. I utilized short quotes and statements from the group and individual interviews to inform the phenomenological study and to analyze the college choice process of Latina transfer students. And even though I thought I did a fair job of capturing the college choice process in a comprehensive manner, I remained curious about the success stories I had heard. I wondered if I fully articulated the meaning behind their stories and if I adequately conveyed the realness in their voices to depict the breadth and depth of their experiences.

While I am pleased with the data analysis and the discussion in my study, the personal narratives from the interviews stood out in my mind as a potential source of inspiration and motivation for students currently in the throes of their own college choice process. The potential impact these stories could make was on my mind long after I submitted my dissertation for publication and to the university library for circulation. The stories I heard were poignant, raw, touching, emotional, and most importantly, relatable! These lingering thoughts kept nagging at me. Oh, how I wished more students and more educational leaders could be exposed to these personal stories! Eventually this nagging turned into a driving force leading me to convert the interview data I had collected into coherent, connected, and contextualized personal stories that I could share with a wider audience.

One sunny day in September, when the sky was a striking cerulean, I did it. I opened The Box. It was a dust-covered storage bin in the back of my closet that contained all my notes, transcriptions, drafts, concept maps, chapter outlines, drawings, charts, reflective journal entries, articles, and research material from my original study on Latina transfer students. Five years had passed since I last laid eyes on my research. I tried to push aside the distasteful memory of the frustration, mental anguish, and tedious editing nightmare of putting together my dissertation for publication. It was such an ordeal trying to understand how to use Microsoft Word to insert page numbers after a page break and the tab placement for my table of contents in my attempt to address the aperture in the research on meaning and college choice of Latina transfer students.

What could possibly compel me to repeat going through that emotional roller coaster that is the journey of writing a book again? The undeniable fact was that the stories kept calling my name. They waited patiently for me to be ready and now was the time to bring these stories to light. I re-read the transcriptions from all my interviews. I re-read my interview notes. Along the way I asked myself several questions. Where these stories really as powerful as I had remembered? Are the stories still relevant and relatable to students today? Were the interviews good enough to stand on their own? Did they stand the test of time? As I re-read the stories, I recalled the outpouring of emotions from the students as they recalled their stories of the journey to completing their baccalaureate degree. Their words painted such vivid pictures with the use of humor, imagery, memories and conversations. What also struck me was how often my own experience overlapped theirs, how intertwined our histories, re-alizations, and perceptions were, as if braided together to create this tapestry of meaning. Like threads of yarn interwoven to form a patterned blanket, the stories provided an opportunity for knowing and understanding the college choice process from the students' point of view. These stories are a way to under-stand their ways of being as Latina transfer students at a com-munity college. It is no wonder that these stories have influenced me in such a deep, personal, and profound way. I experienced such a visceral reaction to these stories. I anticipate others will as well.

These stories can positively impact students as well as par-ents going through the college choice process, whether or not students are considering the community college or the univer-sity route. My hope is to honor the study participants by sharing their stories in their entirety so others may take solace in know-ing that they are not alone on this journey toward a college ed-ucation. Let this book provide a source of hope for high school and community college students as well as a call to action for educational leaders in all sectors of higher education.

Not only are the voices of the students important in their own right, but it is a critical time in the United States' history when voices of marginalized groups are being silenced and de-monized. The year 2016 is marred by one of the most contentious

United States presidential elections in recent history. This election underscores the ugly reality of racism, sexism, xenophobia and other hateful aspects of society that cannot go ignored. The present day accusatory rhetoric is a harbinger for uncertain times in our country. There is heated debate over personal freedoms, domestic and foreign policy, immigration policy, workforce development, and the differences between the haves and have-not's continues to only get wider and wider. The political unrest means our nation and our youth are looking for guidance and support from our social institutions, including our educational system.

Most importantly our youth are making their way in the world today using strategies, ideas, and pathways that simply did not exist ten years ago. Yet, even in our rapidly changing world, a college education continues to be the best path for cultural, social, and economic advancement. Especially with the constantly changing social, economic, and technological environments, a college degree continues to offer the surest route toward exploration, experience, and preparation for our best and brightest minds.

Finally, with the expense of higher education continuing to skyrocket, the community college remains the de facto entry point for higher education for many families. More than ever before, our students deserve to have access and opportunity to fully participate in our global society. Though our students come with diverse life experiences, including those who are entrepreneurial, low income, immigrants, refugees, religious minorities, LGBTQI, military veterans, single parents, differently abled, English language learners, first generation, academically talented, older, and non-traditional in every sense of the word, the doors to higher education must remain steadfastly wide open. We must welcome all our students with arms wide open. The opportunity we have before us is the ability to usher in a new epoch of higher education policy that is relevant and inclusive of the students we strive to develop as citizens of our local and global communities. Now. More than ever. We owe it to ourselves and our future generations to lift every voice.

Chapter One

Introduction

The thought of going to college can raise many questions. Students and parents alike often ask similar questions: How and when do I get started? How can I afford it? Is it worth it? Who can help me with my essay? What are the deadlines? What about my SAT/ACT scores? Is my GPA good enough? How hard are the classes? How do I choose the right college? Do I choose a major or career first? What if I am the first in my family to go to college?

For students thinking about going to a community college, they often ask the above questions plus some. The most common questions, by far, are: How do I make sure I don't get stuck? How can I transfer in two years? How do I get out as soon as possible? Nobody wants to get stuck at a community college!

When you are Latina and going to a community college, you might have more specific questions. How can I help my family pay bills while I go to college? Can I go to college if I am an undocumented immigrant? How can I help my parents understand that I might need to study at the library all night? Who can help me explain to my family why as Associate's Degree is not enough? How can I help my family understand that going away to college does not mean I am walking away from my family or culture?

The personal stories in this book come from Latina students who figured out the answers to these questions and more. These stories come from Latina students who did not get stuck in community college. Assuredly, there were times when they doubted themselves and their goals. They worried about asking for too much out of life. At times, they thought they might be testing fate. But each story demonstrates how they transferred from the community college to some of the best universities in the world. They found their inner strength with their family by their sides and their sense of self-determination by taking charge of their life. They did not allow anything or anyone to get in their way. They found out how to make the life they wanted by counting on no one but themselves. There are lessons here for every student making the choice of whether or not to go to college.

Most importantly, these personal stories represent the unique and diverse perspectives within the Latina Diaspora. There are nine personal stories of transfer from a California community college to a world-class university. Learn how these students made the decision and fulfilled their transfer dreams of going from the community college to campuses in the University of California system, the California State University system and private universities.

The first narrative is about getting over the stigma of attending a community college. Belleise is a student from a middle-class suburban family. She did everything right in high school, taking honor classes and earning over a 4.0 GPA. She fits the perfect description of someone who would traditionally attend a four-year university straight after high school. At first she attended a private high school. She knew all about college admission requirements early in high school. She took advantage of the Early Decision admission option and was admitted to UC Santa Barbara. Everything seemed to go according to plan until one of her parents was diagnosed with a life threatening illness. In an instant, her college plans went out the window. Instead of attending the university by the sea, Belleise found herself attending the community college down the road. She dreaded the idea of being a community college student. It was one of her worst nightmares come true! Find out how she eventually came to the realization that attending community college was one of the best decisions she could have ever made in her life.

In the following chapter, there is the story of a Latina student athlete who learned to solve her own problems on and off the field. Playing soccer was what drew Paula to college. She could not wait to play on the college soccer team! Her high school soccer coach got a job at a local community college and she was recruited along with a few of her friends to play there. The problem began when her coach was let go. In the search to play for a new team, Paula transferred to a different community college to complete her second year of athletic eligibility. While she loved playing soccer and completed all her college classes, Paula was not an all-star athlete. She received no guidance or attention once her eligibility to play soccer ran out. She eventually learned to focus her attention and get her priorities straight. This chapter highlights the importance of asking questions and seeking help when you no longer have a coach to guide you.

In *Breaking Stereotypes*, Sapphire is the first in her family to go to college. She knew she was destined for college early in life. As an honors' student since junior high school, there was tremendous pressure for Sapphire to succeed. She felt like a token minority, forced to excel because learning came easy to her. The pressure of stress in school proved too much. Rather than applying to college, Sapphire did the unexpected. She enlisted in the United States Marine Corps. After serving her country for four years, she returned to pursue higher education. She chose community college to save money and to remain close to home. While in community college, she was active on the cheer squad, president of multiple student clubs, and involved in the civil rights-themed community service project *Mendez v. Westminster*. In this chapter, Sapphire talks about the importance of not settling and of the important of demanding more from yourself and the college when it comes to reaching your goals. Sapphire is an excellent example of a person who never compromised on reaching her highest goals.

Chapter five is about Dahlia who graduated high school with a 1.8 GPA. She had no idea what would become of her life after high school. She enrolled in community college mainly so she could take a job as a student worker. Little did she know, but along with the job, Dahlia would find a complete support system through the EOPS program. Her counselor became a father figure who guided her every step of the way. From her first day on campus, Dahlia knew she loved community college! In this chapter, Dahlia discusses how she went through a complete personal transformation as a result of attending community college. While before she was consumed by intense self-doubt, ultimately she gains a sense of confidence that completely changes how she sees herself and her future. See how Dahlia's community college experience transformed her sense of self.

It's so Mexican! is about Anais and her cohort of high school friends who decided as a group to enroll in community college after graduating from high school. Seven clever friends mapped out their classes as a group and traded books to save money. They attended community college in order to build up their academic skills and their confidence in preparation to take college level coursework. Anais came from a family where no one discussed college planning. Her home life was not as supportive as she would have liked. Even so, her family expected her to complete post-secondary education. She also worked at her father's restaurant since the age of 12 and she knew she had a love for helping others. Along with her friends, she found success by working on campus and learning about college resources. Find out how she used her interest in helping others to identify a college and career pathway that lead to her success.

Next is Desi's story. She is an undocumented immigrant, who earned a 3.5 GPA in high school. She completed Advanced Placement classes and hoped to attend medical school someday.

She thought of herself as her dad's right hand because she came from a single parent household and took on the responsibilities of the mother of the family in raising her baby sister since she was a one year old. After high school, she went to work full-time and attended community college part-time. Each semester, she would register for classes and then drop them. Add classes, then drop classes, semester after semester. She was eventually placed on academic probation. She realized she needed to take control of the decisions she was making in her life. Learn how she developed a council of advisors to help her achieve her goal of transferring from the community college to a four-year university.

In chapter eight, Dana describes the hardship of coming from a family where all the women were teenage mothers. For the longest time, the only goals she had in her life were to get a high school diploma and to not get pregnant. She was in the college preparation program Puente in high school and knew all about college. Yet to her, college seemed like a fantasy world. In the real world, she was facing a difficult home life that included her brother getting sentenced to prison for gang-related activity and her family losing their home. These problems overshadowed her college choice process. Dana suffered from overwhelming self-doubt and depression. She did not feel worthy enough to attend college, especially when she was surrounded by strong Latinas taking care of their families on their own. She eventually learned to accept that she had academic talent and deserved to get a college education. She had to face her fears and to overcome her self-doubt again and again. With the help of her friends, Dana realized it is possible to go to college and that she could serve as a role model to her cousins and the people in her neighborhood. Learn how developing personal connections at the college made all the difference.

In the next chapter, Jaqueline experiences culture shock when she attends community college for the first time. She hails from a tight-knit ethnically monocultural community that is 95% Latino. She eventually gets accustomed to the different ways people dress, talk, and express themselves. Coupled with the culture shock, Jaqueline is insecure about her academic skills. She feels that her high school classes did not adequately prepare her for college level work. She would get physically ill at the very thought of writing a college essay. She achieves more than she ever thought possible by seeking out help and taking an active role in her education. Along the way, she learns to appreciate her family even more for their support and care. Find out how she learned to have patience with herself and how she made progress towards her goals taking it one step at a time.

The final chapter is about Thalia, an undocumented immigrant who learns to be a trailblazer for her family. She participated in the college preparation program AVID during high school and went on different college fieldtrips. But she did not feel a connection to the universities or to her life so she did not consider the option of attending a university after high school. She faced many barriers including being raised by a single parent and being responsible for helping to pay the family's rent. Her father knew very little about the American education system and he did not speak English. She would seek out information about college to take back to her family. She faced multiple obstacles including accepting her sense of self and overcoming her insecurity about her immigration status. Find out how Thalia used critical conversations with her family to make college a priority and how she found an academic family and a place to call her support headquarters at the community college.

All these stories come from a place of wayfinding and meaning making through the transfer maze. Learn how these Latinas cross the border from the community college to the university. These narratives show the importance of having critical conversations with their family, leveraging social capital to develop a network of positive peer pressure, identifying difference makers at the college and the universities, navigating academic land-marks and milestones, and the necessity of developing a new sense of self and their academic potential. The students over-come fear, stigma, self-doubt, and negativity which in turn re-veals a new path forward. Join them on their journey as they transfer not just from the community college to the university, but towards a future different from the one they or their parents ever imagined. Read about how family and culture provide the cornerstone for personal success for these amazing Latina trans-fer students from a California community college.

Chapter Two
Avoiding the Worst Case Scenario

I can't remember back to a time when I actually thought about being in college because with both of my parents working at the community college, the idea of college was always there.

My mom would pick me up from daycare and I'd come back with her to her office on campus. I'd sit in the office with her until she finished her work. Or I would come with her on the weekends when she had a lot of work. I would sit there in the office and watch her. And the days when I was sick. So, to me, I was always on campus. I was always aware of what happens after high school which is going to college.

Another thing is on the weekend; my mom did financial aid presentations, so those were imbedded in my mind since I was a little kid. I don't think I understood what she was talking about until I started working at the college myself. Then I was the person giving those speeches. I recalled the actual setting of my mom standing in front of a lot of people. All these people listening to her, taking down vital information, that to me was all the same thing, Cal Grant, Cal this, Cal that, scholarships. I would be in the background doing my homework. So I was always there.

I started at a private high school. My counselor there spoke to me about college right away. That's another way that I was introduced to the idea. It was always understood that from high school, you go to a university. That counselor was really pushy too. She gave me a schedule of courses to complete during my four years in high school that would get me into a university. That was a good thing because at the public high school, when you're a freshman, I don't even know if they give you a four year plan or not. And usually, it's not the A thru G requirements. So, when I left the private school to attend a public high school, I kept the same A thru G schedule of classes I had planned. That is exactly what I took in high school. So, that's how the environment shaped my views on college.

For me, the community college students I would meet or the stories I would hear is that everyone stays here. Even the students my mom would meet or my mom would talk about. Never in a bad light or anything, but the community college students were always struggling. They were working. They're graduating after so many years with only an Associate's Degree. To me, it was supposed to be four years and you're done with your Bachelor's Degree. The stuff that I would hear from my mom is that students who go to community college had some type of hardship. They didn't know how to study or they didn't have the resources or they weren't determined to finish school. Or it was something they were doing as a favor to their parents, lack of motivation, I guess. That's why I never saw myself at the community college, cuz I thought it's for people who don't know where they're going or for people that have to work and don't have any money. My dad never put us in the position where I thought I had to go to community college instead of a university.

I always pictured that after high school,
I was going to go to a four year university.

My parents were always supportive of me and my college choice. My mom would joke around sometimes like, "Oh, don't go too far. You can do two years at the community college. We'll save money." But it was just a joke. My dad, he always wanted me to go out on my own. On his side of the family, all my cousins have failed at that. They're in their 30's and they're still on his brother's and sister's money. I'm very close to my cousins, so he thought I was going to develop the same bad habits as them. He always pushed me. He would tell me, "Hey, when I was 18, I went across the country. I was by myself. Don't forget that when you turn 18." When I was a junior in high school, I was getting letters from faraway places like NYU, MIT, and Columbia. He was like, "Look at those schools!" And I was like "No! I do not like snow! I'm sorry. I'm staying in California." He was always willing, not overly pushing me, but willing to have me go far away. And usually in the Latino culture dads never let their daughters go anywhere but my dad is totally an exception to that rule.

I thought it was cool. I didn't feel like he wanted me out of the house. I really got it. I really got that his family had a lot of influence over him. They see my relationship with my cousins and they're like, "She's going to end up just like them, if you're as lenient as the other ones. Don't be lenient." I understood where he was coming from but I was like "Look, I'm gonna go to a university. I'm going to do fine. I'm going to do great. I don't have to go across the country for that. I'm not going. I have a mom that I actually want to be around." He would jokingly ask me, "Why don't you want to look?" I would be like, "I don't want to. This has been our problem the whole time we've been living here. I hate the fact that our family is far away. You know that already and me going away is only going to make that worse." I was like, "I always throw it in your face, why didn't you bring the whole family when you were moving to the U.S.? When I feel like coming home, I don't want to have to deal with having to pay for a ticket or the price of a ticket stopping me from coming home. I'd rather be a car ride away rather than transportation being an issue and transportation is an issue now with the family. We only go out to see other family once or twice

a year. I don't want it to be the same with my immediate family."
So he respected me for that. He respected my feelings but he
kept saying, "Keep your options open." I'm like, "There're
awesome schools around here."

My mom never had that opportunity to go away to college
or finish college in general but she was very supportive. She
never said, "Don't go somewhere because I'm going to miss
you." But I knew deep down that I was gonna miss her. She and
I are very close. I told her, "There are other options." I wanted
to live in other places but not permanently. I always want to live
in California. There's an MBA summer internship at NYU in
New York City. I said, "I want to go to New York and experience
that but I do not want to move there yet." There are options,
other options that I've looked at like internships I can do out of
state to expand my worldview. That's what my mom and I talk
about. It's not that I'm closing myself off to California but
California is where I want to live because that's where my family
is. I'll experience and achieve what I want to achieve through
other means. She's always been extremely supportive of what I
want to do.

*While both parents encouraged Belleise to go to the
university directly after high school, her mother was struck with
a very serious illness. So even though Belleise was offered
admission to UC Santa Barbara, she declined the offer of
admission in order to stay close to home and to be with her
mother in her time of illness.*

When I realized I was going to be attending a community
college instead of a 4 year university, I was very resistant. I was
not happy at all! It wasn't a good time in my life. I was so upset!
The problem was I didn't know who to be upset with or what
to be upset at! I was upset at luck cuz I couldn't be upset at my
mom. I couldn't be upset at my dad. My dad was actually like,

"You should still go to Santa Barbara." No one ever told me to stay. I was upset at life, I guess, and the way things worked out.

I was sitting in the last desk, last chair...
We were both in Honors classes in high school.
We knew we had worked so hard in high school to not be
sitting in that classroom at the community college.
That was how I felt that first semester in community college.

I told my mom if I'm going to stay and go to the community college, then I'm going to work because the classes are most likely going to be easy. I'm going to be bored with my time. I'd rather work as much as I can these next two years because once I get to the university I might not have the luxury to be bored and work. I wanted to work.

Previously, I was working as a swim coach at the gym. I liked that job but I had quit because I thought I was going to go to UC Santa Barbara. I remembered that they really liked me at the gym. My plan was to go back there and work as a swim coach. My mother said "Well, maybe you can get a job on campus. Lots of students do that." So, I was like, "Okay."

The Office of Special Programs ended up hiring me in July before the fall semester. I started there and right away I met a couple of students. They told me about the Honors Program. So I signed up for the Honors Program. I said, "Okay, maybe I'll go to UCLA."

I was getting my feet wet slowly by meeting other students at the college. I knew a couple of people by the time school started but I was still very ugh, you know? I didn't want to be here.

At first, I was very reluctant to get involved,
cuz I just wanted to work and save as much
money as I could and then transfer.

Then, I took my first class. It was an Ethnic Studies class with Professor Adela Lopez. My first semester and Yasmin was in that class – and all the friends that I would end up making! I didn't even know them yet. I was sitting in the back of the room. They were sitting all the way in the front. I was sitting in the last desk, last chair. There was another student who I knew from high school in the class with me. He and I would sit there in the back. He was another person who was not in the best of moods either because he was admitted to the same university as me. But he was an AB 540 student [undocumented immigrant] and he ended up not going.

One day at work, my co-workers were talking and said, "Hey, you know, Erica Bennett is an instructor and she needs help on a film project. The Mendez vs. Westminster Project. Karen says she'll help us with flexible schedules to help her." I said, "No, I don't really want to do that. I'll just be in here in the office." As the week went by I realized there's only so much to be done with the time in the office and then you start to get bored. So I said, "Maybe I'll switch my hours to help on that project. It can't be any harder than sitting in the office filing paperwork." So I switched my hours and started to volunteer with Professor Erica Bennett. I said right away, "I'm not going to be on camera." They said I could be assistant director. And as assistant director I had to sit with her and interview all these students. Professor Adela Lopez had sent her students to volunteer for credit. The first person we interviewed was Yasmin and then the second person was Sapphire. So on and on it went and then when we had class that following Monday. I saw Yasmin again and I was like,

> "Aren't you the girl we just interviewed?"
> And she was like, "Yeah".
> And I was like, "I didn't know you were in my class."

And so, after that day, we started hanging out every day. And then, from there, we would have class, then we would have practice for the play. Then I would have time off. One time I asked,

"Where are you going?"
She says, "Oh, a MEChA meeting"
I'm like, "What's that?"
She says, "Just come, come on, just come."

She and Sapphire, they had already been on campus for a year. They had been the presidents and vice presidents of all their clubs. They invited me everywhere, "Come with us, we're going here. Just come with us." So I started getting dragged along to all these things and before I knew it, I was really involved. And doing the tables, "Oh, watch the table while we go to class." And I was like, "Okay." They would see me sitting outside of my mom's office, waiting for her to get off work around 4:00pm. They had a late class. They would say, "What are you doing?" They'd see me waiting. "Oh, just waiting for my mom to get off work." "Oh! Come with us to get food" or "Come with us. We have to talk about the food drive." "What's the food drive?" And then the following year, I was the one organizing it! So, it just worked out. I met the right people. People that were already involved and before I knew it, I was involved too. And then when they were getting ready to transfer, they were like, "Why don't you run for MEChA club president?" and I said, "No, I'm not gonna. Why am I gonna do that? It's one thing to come to the meetings and sit here. It's another to be in charge of a whole club. No." And they're like, "Well, it's just the same people, come on!" You don't have to sign up for the position of president, they're just, "I volunteer so-and-so to be president..." Then somebody's like, "I second the nomination." And then before I knew it, I was elected! I was like, "Wait!" And they're like, "No, it's not that bad. You'll be fine. Adela's there." And I was like, "Okay, alright."

I remember in high school, I was always really scared to try things. I had a lot of self-doubt. I never volunteered for clubs. I signed myself up to be in clubs but I never volunteered for any leadership positions. Sapphire and Yaz forced me, it was mostly Sapphire cuz she was the one that was leaving. It was her last year. She's like, "We need spots to be filled. Do you see anybody else here to do it?" She's like, "It's not that hard." Before I knew it, I was involved in all this stuff and I liked it.

That was in March. Then in July, right before Sapphire transferred away to the university, and before the semester started here, she said, "By the way, you know that the MEChA President organizes the food drive, right?" And I was like, "What?! No, you guys did not tell me that." She's like, "Yeah, its tradition. That's why Yasmin and I did it last year." When she said that, I was like, "Aw, damn it!" That whole semester I'm going to be so stressed. I started thinking of everything that they had to do for the food drive. That's what I get for leaving early. I remembered how Adela told us all we had to be there for two hours. I remember I wanted to leave as soon as those two hours were over. Sapphire and Yasmin said, "No, you're our friend, so you have to stay and help. The food drive doesn't end until 5:00 in the afternoon." And I said, "Alright, I have to go to the bathroom." But really, I left to go play basketball with my friends instead. So now, this is what I get. I ditched the food drive and now I'm the one who has to organize the whole thing.

It all slowly happened, all my leadership positions. But it helped because this time around I'm already signing up for leadership positions at my transfer school. I'm not even there yet.

*They're like, "You do this program along with your general ed
and you're practically guaranteed a spot at UCLA."
I said, "Okay that sounds good. I'll do that. It's close to home.
I'll be around if anyone needs me. I'll be achieving my
dreams at the same time. That sounds good."*

I remember in high school, I was always really scared to try things. I had a lot of self-doubt. I never volunteered for clubs. I signed myself up to be in clubs but I never volunteered for any leadership positions. Sapphire and Yaz forced me, it was mostly Sapphire cuz she was the one that was leaving. It was her last year. She's like, "We need spots to be filled. Do you see anybody else here to do it?" She's like, "It's not that hard." And so before I knew it, I was involved in all this stuff and I liked it.

As far as getting ready to transfer, during my first year at community college, I told myself I wanted to go to the University of California. I've always wanted to be around the LA area because I wanted to work for the Los Angeles Lakers. That is why I agreed to go to Santa Barbara when I was a high school senior. Because well one, that was the only school I was accepted to as far as the UC. And two, the Lakers hold their summer camp for children in the city of Santa Barbara. So I figured there was some type of connection there.

Originally my plan was to get into UCLA and then to do an internship with the Lakers. When I got to community college, the Office of Special Programs introduced me to the Honors Program. They told me about the statistics for getting into UCLA by completing the program. Right away I signed up. This was in July. The fall semester hadn't even started yet. It was as soon as I got here. And that's how I left it. I made sure to always meet with a counselor cuz stuff was confusing. I saw my counselor, Karen, she was the Honors Counselor. Karen helped me with my AP stuff so that I could get college credit. I saw a counselor every semester, sometimes twice. If I saw that there was a counselor here in the Transfer Center, I would double check just to double check. So, I always had my transfer plans in mind. Four semesters was all I was going to do here. Maybe summer and stuff, but I was always counting, like, "Okay, how many classes do I need? I can do this many if I do summer school to have less." That's why I was so surprised and shocked and upset when Sapphire told me that I was responsible for the food drive right before the semester started.

I didn't plan for that. I had 17 units that semester so I was like, "Oh, I could have taken a lighter load. I ended up dropping a class. I had registered to take calculus. I ended up dropping that so it didn't end up being that bad, but I had my classes in mind when I was doing other stuff. It has always been my classes come first. Then I can handle or incorporate everything else. So since day one, I was thinking, "Okay, I'll be here two years. I'm going to work this many months. Then I'll be taking this many classes each semester. And all the other stuff is just extra."

I always thought of college as a time to go away.
Do something new.

The worst part was at the very beginning, when I first came to the community college. I had a hard time getting past the negative stereotype of people who attend community college. My high school played down going to a community college a lot too. I was in AP classes. I was with students that were in the IB program. I couldn't be in the IB program because I transferred into that school but they had my name on a bulletin board announcing to everyone that I was going to UC Santa Barbara. So my high school classmates were surprised, "You're going to community college? What are you doing?" Everyone expected me to go to Santa Barbara.

What helped me the most at the beginning was making

friends. I didn't know anyone at first. I didn't have any friends, so it was easy for me to draw on that to get new friends.

Something else that helped was as soon as I realized I was going to community college and started working on-campus, I found out about the Honors Program. To me it was the simplest thing ever. Take the Honors courses with your general ed. and I'll be in UCLA in two years. So, it wasn't very difficult for me.

I knew I wanted to apply to UCLA. I had backups just in case I didn't get in. I had about five schools I wanted to apply to. I applied to Berkeley just to see if I could get in because I didn't get in the first time around. It was Berkeley, LA, Irvine. Irvine was the real option, the real second option and then Cal State Fullerton, just in case. I didn't apply to Cal State Fullerton my senior year in high school because I wanted to force myself to go to the UC. UC Santa Barbara was the only school I got into. I was admitted in September thru early decision. So I went through the whole UC application process with my seat already at Santa Barbara. This second time, I was going to apply to all these UC's Berkeley, Davis, LA, Irvine. And Cal State Fullerton. I charged my dad five schools at this point.

The first time I applied I said, "Okay, if I don't get admitted anywhere else, I'm going to go to Santa Barbara." My mom said, "Do Cal State Fullerton, just in case." And I said, "No! I know if I apply to Cal State Fullerton and I don't get into any other place, I'm going to end up at Cal State Fullerton. I don't want that." I always thought of college as a time to go away. Do something new. It would just be more of the same. Everyone that goes to my high school goes to Cal State Fullerton.

The second time around, I also applied to USC. Just to see if I'd get in. I didn't really like the school. Then Cal State Fullerton, because when everything happened with my mom, I said, "I should have applied to Cal State Fullerton." I was just like, "Ugh, I wouldn't be at a community college if I had listened to my mom and applied." And so I said, "I'm not going to let that happen again. I'm not going to spend another year here either, cuz I'm done." I said, "That's not going to happen again. I'll go to Cal State Fullerton and that's the end of it." So I made sure I applied to Cal State Fullerton this time but basically if I had my way, UCLA. That was it but I had backups. For my main school, I knew I had the Honors Program and everything. So, I wasn't stressing about the applications.

I fell in love with the school just by the website!
I saw myself there already! I saw myself taking courses.
I was like, "This is the school I need to be at!"

The university I actually transferred to didn't even come into my mind until December. I had visited UCLA. I tried to make it my new home. A university representative from UCLA would invite me and my friends to campus events. Come to this event or come to that event. We'd go. I liked it but I didn't see myself there. There was a lot of self-doubt and I knew that. I would walk around and people were walking with their face in a book or not talking to anyone. With my friends, you hear us coming from far away. So socially, it wasn't a place I saw myself. But I ignored those thoughts because I always doubted myself. I was like, "I can make it here if I want to make it here. I'll be fine." I ignored it. But I always had that doubt in the back of my mind.

Then one day I was helping Professor Lopez clean her office out. It was December already. All my applications were done. Adela was like, "Belleise, what is your GPA?" I was like, "My grades were just posted. I got a 4.0." She's like, "Why aren't you looking at private schools?" I was like, "Cuz I don't like private school. I had a horrible experience with private school in high school. I don't need to go there again." I thought she was talking about USC. USC has the same school colors as my private high school. There's also a street that runs into USC with the same name as a teacher that I disliked the most at my high school.

Those are all signs. I would be miserable there. And she's like, "That's not the only private school." I'm like, "No, I don't like Chapman; there's nothing there for me. There's nothing that calls my attention." And I kept on cleaning her office. She had hurt her back and all she could do was sit there. She's like, "You know what? Keep cleaning. I'm going to look because there're so many grants, scholarships out there for private schools because the economy is really bad right now." I'm like, "I don't know." She's like, "Well, you clean and I'm gonna look for scholarships. I will send them to your email. You can open them or you can decide not to open them." I'm like, "Okay, that's fine. Sounds good." I didn't want to be mean. Then I finished cleaning.

The next day I opened up my email. The first email I see from her is about Loyola Marymount. And I'm like, "No. Too religious." Then the next one is Chapman and I'm like, "No." My mom always told me they have really bad financial aid. They never meet unmet need. They have this secret rule or whatever that they don't tell students. But the most they meet is like 20 percent or something like that. Something really low. They never strive to meet the full thing. So, I'm like "No to Chapman, my mom would not approve." Then the third email was Pepperdine. I remember looking at Pepperdine when I was in high school but I thought private and I saw how much it was. Then I opened the email and visited the website. I fell in love with the school just by the website! I saw myself there already! I saw myself taking courses. I was like, "This is the school I need to be at!" I even went a little bit crazy about it. She sent me the information about the merit scholarship. She's like, "There is some money here." And I started researching and then I left for Mexico on holiday with Pepperdine on my mind.

*I thought, "Please not the worst school in the world,
not the worst school in the world." When I got admitted to
Santa Barbara, I was like, "Hey, that is not the worst school
in the world, so life is good."*

When I came back I was like, "Okay, I really need to do this. When is the application due?" It was 5 days from now. I was like, "Oh, shoot! I need to do it now!" It happened so fast. That was it. After that, I didn't even want to follow up with Berkeley. I felt like Pepperdine's it. And I remember saying that. Vince, in the Transfer Center, was like, "No, you need to do your Berkeley update." And I was like, "Yeah, but it is so complicated." Deep down I knew I was going to be admitted to Pepperdine. That's where I was going.

At that point, I didn't want to do any of the updates for any of the UCs. Vince was like, "Do it!" And I'm like, "Okay." Vince sat there with me and did the Berkeley update with me. And then John made me do the updates for the rest of them. USC, I didn't even finish following through. They kept hounding me to send all this extra stuff and I just didn't. USC was the one I stopped responding to first. With everyone else, I finished. I completed the updates because they were free but USC wanted me to send them extra stuff that I had to go request and pay money. My AP scores, etc. So I was like, "No. I know for a fact that I don't want to go there."

In March, I started experiencing a lot of self-doubt again. I really saw myself at Pepperdine. It was horrible. I needed a second, back-up plan. I've always had back-up plans. I always ended up with the back-up plans instead of my first choice.

I'm good at that. I always console myself before something bad happens. I'm like "Okay, if UCLA doesn't work out then you'll go to Santa Barbara again cuz you'll most likely be accepted to Santa Barbara then you'll figure out the Lakers thing from there." In March I was like, "Okay, there is no back-up plan here."

I had my heart set on Pepperdine! I never felt that way about a school before. I even told Yaz. I said, "You know, I've never had a dream school." You see families that say, "My kids are going to go to UCLA and UCLA only" or whatever school. They have their hearts set on whatever school. I never had that. My dad wanted us to go to college and that was it. I always approached the topic of a university and a lot of other things in my life as not to aim for the highest but to avoid the lowest. If I have avoided the lowest problem, no problem, but I look at the worst case scenario. If I can avoid the worst case scenario then I made it.

To me I thought, "Please not the worst school in the world, not the worst school in the world." When I got admitted to Santa Barbara, I was like, "Hey, that is not the worst school in the world, so life is good."

I never had my heart set on any school. When I first met Yazmin that was the conversation. I said, "I heard about getting into UCLA with the Honors Program and the statistics. That is definitely not the worst case scenario. I'll just go there." But I never had that feeling of "Oh my gosh, I wanna go there!" The way other students talk about their university or when my dad took me on college tours during my senior year of high school. He told me, "You know, you're lucky that we get to do this, that we can visit universities because when I was young, I never saw my school until I got there. It was across the country. We couldn't go visit." He's like, "I signed up and got accepted and went there." He's like, "but it worked out because the first time I stepped foot on campus, I knew this was my campus. I got that feeling like this is where I need to be." He took me to so many schools. He would be like, "Did you get the feeling? Did you get the feeling?" And I would be like, "No."

I kept to my theory. As long as it's not the worst case scenario, I'll be fine. And then with Pepperdine, it was somewhere in March. I was like, "Oh my gosh! I got the feeling!"

Turned out, I was like my dad! I got the feeling! That was where I wanted to go. I remember in December, we were driving back from Mexico. It wasn't with my mom or my sister. The 14 hour drive and me and my dad were talking about schools. I told him, "Well, Pepperdine is $50,000 and UCLA is $30,000." I guess he heard it in my voice, how I was talking about Pepperdine. He was like, "You really like that school don't you?" And I was like, "Yeah." And he said, "Don't make your decision based on cost." I kept telling him, "My heart's not on Pepperdine. I'm going to go with whatever school gives me the most money and that's it." And he said, "Well, you don't need to focus on the money." He's like, "Let your mom and I worry about that. You go wherever you want to go. Wherever." He's like, "Remember what I told you. That I had that feeling of where I saw myself at that school?" I was like, "Yes, I do." He's like, "Well, you know, just keep looking for that feeling. You have to go somewhere where you're gonna feel comfortable." And I said, "Okay, okay" but in the back of my mind, I was like, "No." This was in December, I thought to myself, "I'm going to go to the school that gives me the most money."

I started doing the application for Pepperdine and looking at all the stuff they offered, then I decided to go on a campus tour. I told myself, "You need to stop because you're in love with the school and you've only seen the website. You've never been on campus." I set up the tour and my self-doubt was like. "You probably won't like the school. Here you got your hopes worked up for nothing. It probably looks like any other school, like UCLA. It's going to be another school."

My mom went with me. We get there and even the security guard at the front gate who gave us the parking permit was really nice. We messed up parking. The parking lot took quarters. The security guard gave us a quarter and we put it in the wrong stall. So I was like, "Shoot are they going to charge us again?" And the guy, he didn't charge us; he just gave us more quarters to put in. I was like, "Oh well, that was nice." I thought we were going to get a ticket or something. Then we went the wrong way to the Admission's Office and got lost. It was just a mess. I'm like, "Mom, what if this is a sign?" And she's like, "Stop it with your signs!"

The tour guide was a university student and there was one more family that signed up for the tour. It was four of us. He took us around. I noticed that as soon as we walked out the double doors, students on campus would greet us.

We finally get to the Admissions Office. I was thinking it was going to be a campus tour with like 70 people, like how it is at UCLA or any other school. I had been on many college tours with my dad. I had a mindset already of what the tour was going to be like. The tour and the informational sessions.

We get to the location we're supposed to be at. It was on the second floor of an administrative office. It was like a reception room for a hotel or something. And the lady said, "Have a seat while we wait for the rest to arrive." We're sitting there and there's like ocean wave music playing in the background. The lady said, "There are some refreshments there for you if you'd like." It's not like they took it out for that day either, they always have refreshments available. And there's a little closet for tea. Tea is my favorite. I was like, "Mom, tea!" and she's like, "Oh, coffee!" We helped ourselves and then we went back to sit down.

There was a touch screen computer showing a virtual campus tour. It came up on the big screen. There was a message from the university president, "Welcome! I'm sorry I couldn't see you in person but I want to personally welcome you to our school." Along with the waves from the beach. The whole time there was ocean wave music playing. I'm like, "Oh, my gosh!"

It was on my mind way too much. Then finally that Saturday, I checked my email. I had the admissions notification that I was accepted. I was like, "Oh my gosh!"

Then our tour guide came in the room. I thought he was a student at the university. He said, "Okay, we're going to go ahead and start. The other families should get here soon." I'm like, "Okay." He's like, "We're going to do the informational session first. We're going to take you to the back." We go through these double doors. The guy was actually not a student; he was an admission's counselor. Mr. Tucker, I think his name was. He took us to his office. I said, "Where is the informational session?" And he was like, "Oh, this is it." It was just my mom and I and the admissions counselor. I was expecting a room with a PowerPoint presentation and 90 seats. And then he's like, "So what questions do you have about the school?" And I was like, "How do I get admitted?" He answered simple questions. He's like, "If we're done, I'll take you to your tour guide now."

The tour guide was a university student. There was one more family that signed up for the tour. It was four of us. He took us around. I noticed that as soon as we walked out the double doors, students on campus would greet us. Students were walking with their faces up. Talking with friends, they didn't have their faces in books like they did not want to talk to anyone. In the cafeteria, it was loud with people talking. The cafeteria was not loud at UCLA. Every table had one person in it with books. And no one was sitting with anyone, no one was socializing. I remember it seemed really cut throat. And the environment at Pepperdine seemed so friendly and welcoming. The complete opposite. In my head went my self-doubt. Still I was like, "I'm in love with this school now. This is definitely where I see myself." When I got home, I told my dad. I told him everything. How great the experience was and by March that's when I realized that's the only school I wanted to go to.

I got mad at myself. I was like, "Why haven't I thought of a back-up plan? This isn't going to work out how I need it to." And I started doubting myself a lot. I'm going to be so disappointed with myself if I don't get accepted there. It's going to be one of my biggest disappointments in my life. I thought up to then the biggest disappointment for me was not going to Santa Barbara but my heart wasn't set on Santa Barbara. It was the idea of going away to college. An accomplishment after graduating high school with a 4.0 then going to a university, which is more than any of my cousins ever did. So, that's something that I was very proud of for myself. Then I told myself, "If I don't get in, this is going to be a bigger disappointment than high school."

I take a while to verbalize many of my doubts. By the time I say them aloud, they've been on my mind for a very long time. It started in March. It was in late March. I started talking about it the first week of April. Mostly with my mom and Yaz, I was like, "You know what? I don't know what I'm going to do. I want to go there. I love everything about that place." And they're like. "Girl, you're going to get in. Don't worry." I was like, "No, you guys need to help me with a back-up plan." It was on my mind way too much. Then finally that Saturday, I checked my email. I had the admissions notification that I was accepted. I was like, "Oh my gosh!"

It was April 2nd because I was admitted for what seemed like a long time compared to the UC's. Then I got the merit scholarship. That was mid-April. The merit scholarship came about 15 days after the acceptance. This whole time, January through March, I had my heart set on Pepperdine. And then, when I had to submit the Statement of Intent to Register, I was like, "No, I can't do it. This is so life changing! I have to wait for UCLA." Then by the time UCLA finally came around, I had already submitted my SIR to Pepperdine.

*This whole time, January through March, I had my heart set
on Pepperdine. And then, when I had to submit the Statement
of Intent to Register, I was like, "No, I can't do it.
This is so life changing!"*

I didn't have a hard time deciding between UCLA and Pepperdine. But still, I thought to myself, "I need to do the x-y chart." The positive and negatives of each school. So I did it. I told myself, I did the Honors Program, so I'm going to think as if I got admitted to UCLA. I did my pros and my cons. Pepperdine ended up on top. I thought to myself, "What if I'm admitted to both schools now what?" The list for Pepperdine came out way longer. I'm like, "Okay, I'm going to submit the SIR to Pepperdine." The SIR required a tuition down payment of $750, when usually it's about $300 for the UCs. I asked my dad for his credit card info and he's like, "Are you 100% that you want to go there because my money does not need to go to waste." I'm like, "Well I'm 99% sure." And he's like, "No, I need you to be 100%. I'm not going to give you the credit info until you are 100%." And I was like, "Okay, I'll come back to you then." And that's when I did my list. And then I went back to him. I said "I'm 100%."

I remember exactly what was on my list. Location was #1. Pepperdine is in the suburbs. LA is so densely populated. There's already so much chaos in my mind. I don't need my college setting to be exactly the same. When I was at Pepperdine, everything was so peaceful. So, it would be great. I knew the school would be great for me mentally. Right off the bat, mentally. And then came the classes.

Obviously, the most important thing on my list wasn't the location; it was the classes and what it had to offer. Pepperdine offered me a Laker internship, not with the Laker's obviously but there was a mandatory internship requirement to graduate. The minor I wanted in Non-profit Management required an internship as well. They were requiring me to do what I always wanted to do. I liked that. And then, I loved the fact that it was a semester calendar and that the teachers were teaching the courses. I never liked how at the UC's one day there is a lecture with the professor and one day there is a section with the TA. I've never liked that schedule. When I heard that the classes were always taught by the professors, I really liked that.

The actual classroom setting was a lot better than the UC system too. I do well in either style of classroom setting but I thrive better in the one where the professor is constantly giving us the attention we need instead of leaving us on our own to figure things out. I can do either way but the way I enjoy it and the way it will stick in my mind so I can have conversations about the topic three years later is in the first style. Right away I was like, "Whoa, this is what I like!"

They told us how the professors talk to students one-on-one. They're given a stipend to take students out to lunch even. It's not weird for your professor to invite the students to their house. To do classes over lunch. It was a little intimidating cuz obviously it's not for the slacker. I've never been a slacker. The best classes I've had here are the ones where I talk with the professors. When I see them at the cafeteria, "Oh, Mr. Powers, how are you doing?" So, to me, I really liked that. I said it's going to be like my Honors classes that I took at community college. So that was definitely a big plus on the Pepperdine side.

They told us how the professors talk to students one-on-one. They're given a stipend to take students out to lunch even. It's not weird for your professor to invite the students to their house and to do classes over lunch. It was a little intimidating cuz obviously it's not for the slacker. I've never been a slacker.

Then the Merit scholarship information came. Pepperdine wanted to give me $23,000 the first year and $22,000 the next year without having to reapply. UCLA, was offering me $1,000 one year and I had to reapply. My dad said, "Don't think about cost. Don't worry, don't add the money."

Then I looked at UCLA. I asked about the style and the approach that they were taking toward my major. My major was Organizational Communications and at Pepperdine it is very hands-on. There's a theory class that I would have to take and an Intrapersonal Communications course but it had a very hands-on aspect with the internship. At UCLA the major is called Communications Studies. And you're studying a lot of the past and it's more a history major. At Pepperdine it is considered a business major and in the end I hope to either work or own my own non-profit. The non-profit minor was like, "Wow, that's a sign!" I'll end up with more business classes. I wanna run a business, without majoring in business. My limit is calculus. That's why I never majored in business because I wasn't good at math. The requirements for the non-profit management were all the business classes that I would need to know to run a business without the calculus. So I was like, "Oh, I'll be able to own a business, yeah!"

At UCLA I asked about the Laker internship and they said internships are done in the summer; basically internships are not required for my major. Any internship you do has to be done in the summer, or you can do it during the semester but you gotta figure out how you're going to incorporate it with your classes. And at Pepperdine, they work your classes around your internship.

I called asking about the Laker internship, because I saw on the website that the deadline is August 17th. I'm not starting there until August 24th. I thought maybe they're going to tell me that I'm calling too early and to hang up and come bother them once I'm on campus. The internship I wanted started on August 17th. I really wanted that internship. The lady I spoke to said she would help me get that internship. And the girl's like, "Oh no, you're right on track. If you're a junior" she's like, "The Pepperdine deadline for any junior internship is August 30th, which is the first day of class." I'm like, "I wasn't told that. I didn't know." And she's like, "Well, most of the juniors aren't transfers so they already have their internship lined up for the year but you don't, so good thing you were looking at them." I was like, "Well, in that case, let me start scrambling for references and stuff." I had a week to complete everything, which is the same as last time when I had about a week to do the application for Pepperdine! They told me, "Your internship is mandatory so we're going to work with your schedule." While at UCLA, it was gonna to be something that I was going to have to do on my own. In a sense, it wasn't for me and I knew that.

The actual transfer process of stopping and going to a community college was a blessing in disguise because I feel more secure in my identity and exactly what I am all about.

The actual transfer process of stopping and going to a community college was a blessing in disguise because I feel more secure in my identity and exactly what I am all about. I know what I stand for, obviously morals and values were taught when I was young and that wasn't a problem but I learned more about things that I'd like to see happen in the world. Things that I want to volunteer with. Things that I want to do. I'm more secure in myself. When I was 18, I was responsible enough to move out. I was level-headed and mature enough to move out but I wasn't molded with an identity yet. Now I'm ready to say, "Sure, I'll be a mentor. Sure, I'll run for the president position." So, my self-doubt has lessened since then. Doing the transfer process instead of going directly helped me mentally believe in myself more.

My mom is like, "I've always seen that." It is one thing for you to see it and it is another thing for me to feel it. My mom's always told me that but I tell her that she can't be that hard on me because I am the mirror version of her. She believes in everyone but herself. I'm like, "That's your fault for not believing in yourself. If anything, I cheer you on all the time and you cheer me on all the time. But we don't cheer ourselves on." She's like, "Okay, okay, okay I'm going to try harder." I got a lot stronger and a lot surer of myself. So, going to community college was one of the best decisions I could have ever made.

To be successful, you need to be very aware of the consequences of failure. I'm really good at putting myself in other people's shoes. Seeing their point of view to understand things because if you always see things from your point of view it is very ignorant. You're being very close minded. I use that when working with other people. I also use it towards my own life and failure. I don't need to fail to know what it is to fail. I put myself in that position. I step out of myself and say this is what is gonna happen if I fail. I am very aware of what can happen if I fail. And so, to me, I can imagine that's already happened. Then there is my theory of avoiding the worst case scenario. Any time I'm in a new setting. I'm like, "Okay, here's the worst case scenario. Here's failure and here's everything that's gonna happen if the worst case scenario happens so let me run in the opposite direction, you know?"

I always start at the bottom, then I think about my dreams. Like staying at home and getting involved with the wrong crowd and my Laker internship. If I avoided this pile then I've already made it. This is a dream that I'm going after but this one is more important to avoid because it is easier. I can relate that to anything.

For example, I started working out. And to me working out a little bit every day is easier than working out a lot and then stopping 3 months and then getting back into. A little bit every day is easier for me to do than starting all over again cuz it's very visual to me. I see it as being the mountain that I have to climb. To me that seems impossible. But if I have something consistent that I'm little by little working at. Here is my dream. Here's the worst case scenario. Let me start working this way little by little. I'll get there. As long as I'm avoiding my worst case scenario, then I've already made it.

There are places I want to get to but life happens in between. I'm so scared of failure that I just don't even want to get there. I can already feel how horrible it would be to be in that situation. I want to avoid that.

This is what it takes to transfer from the community college. Dedication to school. Time management, definitely. Dedication to your classes first. Having that be the priority and everything that encompasses that. Including getting to know your professor. Doing your homework outside of class. Showing up to class on time. Taking notes during class. All that it encompasses, putting in the needed work and the effort needed to do well in your classes.

Getting involved in the community works the best because then you meet people that are as motivated as you or you end up motivating them and that feels just as awesome.

After that I would say starting a social network, making friends because only going to school and going home isn't fun. You can lose your motivation. That's when a lot of self-doubt comes in. I remember my freshmen year and sophomore year at the private high school, I didn't have many friends. It was school and home, school and home. I didn't have anything else to do, so I got straight A's. I had my focus but that was it. I was very sad because I didn't have anything else. I didn't have anyone to relate to. There was always that self-doubt. I can't do anything. All I can do is class. Developing a social network and fun activities that give back to the community helps. Getting involved in the community works the best because then you meet people that are as motivated as you or you end up motivating them and that feels just as awesome.

Always keep your future plans in mind. I never lost sight of the fact that I was going to transfer in 2 years. I'm really good at enjoying the right now as well as keeping the future in mind. Seeing how my right now actions are going to affect my future consequences. I was involved in a lot of things but I never put off my classes for my extracurricular activities. It was always my classes first. I've always had that as a priority. Getting your priorities straight. Cuz the food drive was difficult but it wasn't something that I couldn't do. I never felt the pressure where I couldn't quit. I knew I could quit and give it to Professor Lopez at any time but I also knew I could handle it. It was stressful but I work well under pressure.

Know your limits and don't be afraid to ask questions. If you don't understand what the counselors are telling you, then go see them again. Get to know the people that you need to know in order to transfer: counselors, the Transfer Center. And use the resources available to you for free. I had the class Statistics. It was the hardest thing ever. I was amazed when I found out that there was a Tutoring Center. I was in there and I used it to the fullest advantage. It helped me. I got an A. And the people were really nice. I was surprised that no one talked about it. My friends were taking math. I was like, "Go to the Tutoring Center! It's so awesome!" I'm in there all the time cause in high school we didn't have that. I'm like, "Oh my gosh, there's a Tutoring Center and it is free!" That was really cool. You can balance work, but its knowing how to manage your time wisely. Never losing sight of your priorities.

I had the class Statistics. It was the hardest thing ever.
I was amazed when I found out that there was a Tutoring
Center. I was in there and I used it to the fullest advantage.
It helped me. I got an A.

If I had the chance to do it all again, I would decide what school I wanted to go to beforehand because if I had known I wanted to go in September, I could have fixed my spring schedule to complete more general education courses. Now I have to do 7 classes of general education at Pepperdine. I found this out in the summer. I tried to take summer school here but I'm at my cap for my units.

As far as being Latina, we need to learn how to reject the negative family comments, to let them fall on a deaf ear. My immediate family is very supportive, including my dad in his own special way, but his side of the family, there's a lot of negative, covert comments that come up. I'm used to them already. It's watered down. I don't really care.

But I have friends, one specific friend, who is younger than me. When she started coming to the community college her family was like, "Hey, you're an adult now. You're 18. You better start working." They want to see money coming in. And I'm like, "No, no, no, come to the community college. Don't listen to your mom. I know she's your mom but listen to my mom." She didn't know what she wanted to study so I recommended the Career/Life Planning class. She loved that class! It totally changed her! Now she knows what she wants to do. And she's a little frustrated cuz she took that class later, her second semester. Now, she signed up for 20 units to try and finish in the 2 years because she has a goal now.

I've always been able to have these dreams and goals that I've wanted to achieve because my family's been supportive. I think she had no idea and no vision because her parents were cutting her off when they're like, "Hey, don't forget that by the time you're 18, you're going to be working." She's never been able to see past that. Now she sees me like an older sister. She's seeing the things that I'm a step away from accomplishing. She has goals now too. And I'm really excited for her. Now she's listening even less to her parents. She's like, "Hey, here is my financial aid money. I can give my family money." I tell her, "Don't give them all your money. You need that!" So, the second time around she used her money more wisely from financial aid and got herself a laptop. Then she gave her parents the money left over. But they're seeing her with her laptop. I warned her, "They're going to get mad at you now but they are going to thank you later because you're going to be making the big bucks."

Maybe we can show Latinas not to teach them to ignore your family but to find a support group at college. Tell them, "Hey, there is another side of that argument. Your parents weren't given that opportunity so they don't know what it is. But you're given this opportunity, so take full advantage of it." A supportive group that would understand where the Latinas are coming from would help more students. And then if they're single parents in college, that's a whole other thing. The Latina culture has a lot to do with it though, lack of support.

Here, it's all up to you. You can come here in your first semester and take 2 classes. That's the worst thing to do! You want to keep on going like its high school and take the 5 classes, take the 4 classes.

Students think that community college is an extension of high school but in high school you're forced to do so many things. Here, it's all up to you. You can come here in your first semester and take 2 classes. That's the worst thing to do! You want to keep on going like its high school and take the 5 classes, take the 4 classes. And then, I don't know if you can make it mandatory to see a counselor but at least let them know it's an option. It's in your best interest. It's all up to you now. You're not going to get a little pink slip that gets you out of class to go see a counselor. You have to do it yourself. In the long run, it's only going to benefit you.

Anytime I hear that anyone is confused of what they want to study, I always recommend that Career/Life Planning class. I only took it because it was offered during winter session. I wanted to be in school. I didn't want to be bored at home. Rolando was teaching it. I'd always see him around. I heard he's funny. So, I took it. I always knew I wanted to study communications so I wasn't lost. But I saw people in that class that were saying, "I don't know what I want to do." When the class was over they were like, "Oh, my gosh! This class changed my life!" It didn't change my life but it emphasized it. The two things that stuck with me: 1. everything pointed at communications, so I was in the right field. And 2. it was so funny. We took this one test that gauges your abilities, skills, what you're good at and what you're not good at. Mine said I was good at absolutely nothing. I had zero skills but the ability was 100%. I have the drive to work hard to learn things. Basically, I know nothing but I have the drive to work very hard to learn everything I want to learn.

That idea always stuck with me. For example, when I was training at the gym for the very first time I did a new exercise. I was horrible at it. The first time, they're like, "Oh, you can't do that!" And then, the second time around, the second rep I was 100% better. So, little things like that happen. I'm like, "That's like the exam that I took that says I have zero skills starting out but I have the ability to work hard enough in order to develop those skills." I remember I didn't understand the results. Rolando kinda laughed at the results. He said, "Well, you can take it one of two ways. You suck at doing everything or you have the ability to develop anything and everything you want to do." And I'm like, "I like the second one a little more."

Every time that I hear someone say, "Oh, I don't know, I don't know," I always recommend a Career/Life Planning class. I'm like, "Take the class. You do all these exams that evaluate what you are like." I started looking at occupations when I was younger, as a sophomore/freshman in high school. A lot of students don't have that advantage. You walk out of that class with a list of stuff that's right for you. And then, you research what you wanna study or what you wanna do as an occupation." People that listened to me and take it come out like, "Yes! Here are 5 things that I want to do now." I get so excited! That's one of the main classes that they should promote more for students that are stuck.

Profile update: Belleise transferred to Pepperdine University by the ocean in Malibu, CA. She graduated with her Bachelor of Arts Degree in Organizational Communication. While a student at Pepperdine, she completed a 9-month internship as a Community Relations Intern with the Los Angeles Lakers. She now works as an Administrative Manager for a non-profit organization in Southern California.

Chapter Three
Internship, work, school, soccer

The thing that I was most excited about in going to college was the idea of being able to play on the college soccer team. I didn't really think twice about going to college because I had two older siblings. They went to college already. So it was the natural next step. It was never like, "Do I want to go? Do I want to take a semester off?" It was just, "Go to college and that's it."

I always knew, since early in life. I'm gonna go to college. What I actually looked forward to most was playing sports.

My parents really wanted us to go to college. They were like, "As long as you go to school, you don't have to pay rent. You don't have to pay for anything. Just continue going to school." Especially my mom. She was really into it, she was like, "Go to college. You don't wanna be like me and not have an education." So it was something that was embedded in me to not even think twice about going to college. I always knew, since early in life. I'm gonna go to college. What I actually looked forward to most was playing sports.

I was excited to go to college because it was something new. I didn't stress out about classes. I knew I did well in class, so I wasn't like, "Oh my gosh." In the beginning, I was like, "Oh, I'm going to college and just go with the flow." I'm the type of person who goes with the flow. And then, probably in my third year in college, I was like, "Okay, I really need to transfer out of here now." I was doing my work, but I was also taking it kinda easy. Plus, I found a full-time job I really liked. Slowly I was drifting from going to college full-time to part-time and then finally one semester I was like, "Whoa, what am I doing?" I stopped. I thought about it and was like, "Okay, my work is not important. My parents aren't even asking for rent money. I don't even know what I'm doing with all my money." I focused more on transferring out because personally the hardest thing is to transfer out. I didn't realize that it gets kind of, "Ugh, I don't want to take this class or that class." It becomes hard. On my own, I was like, "I need to get out of here."

Since my junior year of high school, I knew I wanted to go to a community college. I never took the SATs. I was ready for community college. My oldest brother went straight to university. My sister went to college and then she transferred. So I was like, "Let me get a scholarship. Then I'll go to junior college first 'cuz it's less expensive."

The one thing my parents always enjoyed was for us kids to go to college, go to university, and work on our degrees. So they've always been like, "Go to school. Go to school. Get your degree. If you meet somebody, don't depend on anybody." Especially us girls.

My dad wouldn't really give us a lot of advice but one thing
he would always tell me and my sister was,
"Go to college. Get your degree.
Don't depend on no guy. Do everything on your own."
And my mom, she always had our backs.

My dad wouldn't really give us a lot of advice but one thing he would always tell me and my sister was, "Go to college. Get your degree. Don't depend on no guy. Do everything on your own." And my mom, she always had our backs. I took my parent's advice as, "Go get your degree and be somebody."

I first went to community college because my soccer coaches in high school recruited a few girls from the soccer team. We all went to a community college in a different city. I was there for a semester. And then those coaches got fired, so then I was like, "Well, I'm not gonna go there." Then I came to this community college for my second semester. Then I started my second year of playing soccer.

At this community college, it was a little weird. The campus and stuff. At the other community college, I always had somebody with me. Here, I had to do everything on my own. I had a few friends but I was mostly by myself. Like finding my classes. I didn't have a partner kind of person.

My plan was actually to transfer and play soccer for a university. So I applied at Long Beach and I got accepted there but I also applied to Cal State Fullerton. I don't know why I chose Long Beach but if I had picked Long Beach, I would have tried out for the team there. When I went to Cal State Fullerton, they had a team there but I didn't talk to the coaches or anything. If I had gone to Long Beach it would have been different. Maybe the reason why I transferred over to Cal State Fullerton was because it was closer and my sister went there.

When it was time to transfer from the community college, I went to the Transfer Center and they helped me. They told me about the process for transferring and the application. But I really did everything on my own.

I applied to Long Beach and Cal State Fullerton. Because they were more local than other universities. I didn't apply to the UC's. I had a lot of friends that went there but I had no idea. I don't know why. I did everything on my own.

I don't even know why I applied to Long Beach besides the soccer thing. I was planning to only apply to Fullerton.

I got a hold of the soccer coach at Long Beach State. She wanted me to send her a video of one of my games. Luckily I had a video. I sent it to her. I applied and was accepted. I applied to Cal State Fullerton and got accepted there so I was like, "I'm just gonna go there."

I'd never been to that campus in Fullerton before I applied. It was local and all my friends had transferred there, and my sister went there.

As far as dating, the guys I dated were not the deciding factor. My family weren't involved either. It was just me on my own.

I'd never been to that campus in Fullerton before I applied. It was local and all my friends had transferred there, and my sister went there.

When I did finally transfer, it made me feel like, "See, I can do it." I felt I can achieve something. I can achieve my goals as far as education-wise. I did it! It was really exciting for me when I got accepted into the schools!

For some reason, I thought that I wasn't going to get in. But then I saw how people that went to this community college transferred there. They mostly got in. That was something that kept my hopes up, but I remember thinking I would not get in.

I know there are obstacles that I need to overcome. And there might be some stuff that…you know how sometimes when something goes wrong; it feels like everything else is going to go wrong.

As far as failing, I don't think I had to fail; it just took longer for me to get going. At junior college to transfer, it's not like I was failing, it was just taking more effort than I expected. It was taking more than what I probably thought it was gonna be to transfer out.

I transferred out when I was 23. So it took me 4 years to transfer out. I got into the whole working full-time thing. School was becoming part-time. I was like, "Wait a minute. I don't want to be working here for the rest of my life. I need to go back and focus on school. Get my priorities straight." That was probably the first semester. I was new to the whole college scene. I wanted to party and meet people and socialize. I was working as a receptionist. I got the job through a friend. I would work until 3:30pm. After work, I would go to class. I took the classes in the evening. I had the whole day. Then I would think about it and be like, "Oh, I don't wanna go to class."

I do have an instructor that I still keep in touch with. He actually got me an internship for my degree. I was doing counseling for drug intervention. He's always been somebody I can go to and that I could talk to.

I had a few friends but I was mostly on my own. I did have one or two girlfriends that I would do all my work with. We would do homework together.

To transfer from a community college, you need to have priorities straight and have school as your focus and not be sitting in the back of the classroom. You can socialize and party but remember that you have to do well in your classes. If I could go back, I would change that. Instead of me taking four or five years to transfer out, I would be more focused on that and try to not mingle so much. I would just transfer out.

I really wanted to transfer out but maybe if I'd had a counselor or a professor to talk to maybe it would have helped me snap out of it quicker than I did. I had to snap myself out of it.

I would definitely recommend students talk to counselors but not just anybody. Try to find a counselor that can go there with you. Not just to talk about transferring but somebody that can just talk. If not a counselor, then even a teacher. 'Cuz I really wanted to transfer out but maybe if I'd had a counselor or a professor to talk to maybe it would have helped me snap out of it quicker than I did. I had to snap myself out of it. Maybe a teacher or a counselor would have noticed it sooner. It would have taken me like a year or something.

Also, look into more schools! I could have applied to and researched way more than I did. It doesn't hurt to apply. Look into more than the schools around you to see what else the schools have. At first, I was a sociology major and then I took a human services class and I was like okay, human services. I talked to someone in the human services department, and that's why I went there.

Maybe it would be good for community colleges to have a program where the students can hear from students that already transferred. Someone that already graduated. Someone with a Master's or a Doctorate degree. Let them see that they can do it too.

After I finished playing soccer, I didn't talk to anybody that was on me like, "Oh yeah, transfer out." Even if you aren't the all-star student athlete, there should be somebody that you can talk to, someone to take the time to ask, "Hey, have you ever thought of transferring and playing sports at that university?" I didn't really have that, or have anybody to help me out. It was something I had to do on my own. Because of that, I didn't transfer out to play. Maybe that would have motivated me or inspired me to wanna continue playing soccer. If I had somebody there telling me, "You know what? You should go."

Now I play on a co-ed softball team, no soccer though. I miss it. I really miss it! And I really regret not playing!

It was my internship, and work, and school, and then soccer. It was like that. I didn't give it a chance because I knew it was gonna be hard. I knew it was gonna be very difficult for me to go to school and to have an internship and to work. I was like, "Oh my gosh!" I would probably have to stop working.

My parents don't ask me for much but I have my car. I have my bills so I have to work even if it's part-time. I have to have some kind of income coming in because I can't ask my parents for money. I don't ask my parents for money. Ever since my senior year of high school, I have been working. I pay for my own stuff. The least thing I can do is to pay for my own bills instead of asking my parents. I pay for everything. My classes, my books, everything. I didn't want to ask them for anything. Not because they didn't want to, but because I'm an adult. I have always been working.

As soon as you transfer out, it's the easiest thing!

As soon as you transfer out, it's the easiest thing! Oh my god, two years? Next thing you know you're already graduating. Like wow, that was quick!

Profile update: Paula transferred to Cal State University, Fullerton and graduated with her Bachelor of Arts Degree in Communication – Advertising. She went on to work with athletic organizations including the Rancho Cucamonga Quakes and the Major League Baseball team, Los Angeles Angels. She is currently working as an Account Manager in Southern California.

Chapter Four

Breaking Stereotypes

I was in 10th grade when I realized that college was my destiny. That was when I first had the thought that I *have* to go to college. I did not even have a sense of wanting to go. It was like, "I have to go to college." As an honors' student since junior high school, I was part of a token group that the school focused on. Everybody else was talking about, "When I graduate, I'm going to start working. I am going to work when I graduate." But us token few were like, "Oh, we have to go to college. There's no other choice." Personally, myself, I felt a lot of pressure. That's probably why I didn't go to college right after I graduated with honors from high school.

It seemed like everybody at the high school relied on those token few of us to go to college. It's like, "I don't know what I want for myself. How can I take on all of this also?" It was hard. I envisioned college at the end of a very long, dark tunnel. It's very dim because I knew that I couldn't afford it. I knew that I would have to be working two or three jobs while trying to get through college. And at the same time I was scared to leave home. I knew that I would have to go to Cal State Fullerton or someplace local.

I was going to go to college right after high school. But I wanted more for myself. I wanted to be independent. I felt like if I did go to college with those expectations of remaining close to home, I wasn't going to get to do my personal thing. What I wanted to do. Be free. Be independent. Make my own decisions.

Learn stuff that you can't learn unless you live through it.

When I decided not to go to college straight after high school, my parents were really disappointed at first. My mom expected more from me. My dad thought, "She's gonna graduate high school and go to college." So when I didn't, I think they were disappointed but at the same time I think they understood where I was coming from.

My mom was the main motivation in my decision to join the military after high school. I told her, "When I finish with the military, I promise you, I'm going to go to college." I promised I would do the school thing. The military is going to help me. In a way, she was disappointed I wasn't going to do it right away, but then she was happy and satisfied, knowing eventually I was going to get there. She trusted me. I made the right decision for myself.

My mom trusted me in making my own decisions, which is something that I hadn't had before. Before it was always, "Why don't you ask your mom first?" My mom, before my dad. Up until I was 18, all my decisions were based on my mom. "Can I do this? Can I do that? Oh, I have to ask my mom first."

I had this impression that once you get here, you get sucked in. You can't get out.

After finishing four years with the military, I went to community college. I knew it was going to take a lot of work. I had heard from friends who graduated from high school. They were still here. It was those friends that I would run into when I was on leave from the military. I was home every so often. I'd be like, "What are you doing?" They'd be like, "Oh, I'm still at community college." I had this impression that once you get here, you get sucked in. You can't get out.

My mentality coming to the community college was, "I'm here. I'm going to transfer. I'm not going to get stuck."

I had heard from a lot of my friends, "Oh, I'm still here." I was like, "Weren't you there 3 years ago. Isn't it a 2 year school?" That was my goal. I wasn't going to be here more than two years. Once I came to a transfer event and Vincent was doing his presentation. He said, "On the average, it takes a student three years to transfer." I could not afford three years.

I got a head start by taking college classes
when I was in the Marine Corps.
I earned college credit while I was in the military.

I already postponed college four years by being in the military. I'm thankful for those four years. I became more appreciative of school more so than if I had gone directly to college. I don't think I appreciated my education before as much as I do now. When I heard him say that and because I saw that some of my high school friends were still here, it motivated me. I was determined to not fall in that cycle, "Oh, you're at community college. You're going to be there three-plus years before you transfer." I know myself. No. I can be out of here in two years. I can do it.

I got a head start by taking college classes when I was in the Marine Corps. I earned college credit while I was in the military. That was really helpful because I got the math out of the way. Other courses transferred over unknowingly. Then I found out about the IGETC plan. I had already completed some of the classes!

All the students looked so young to me! I knew I was going to be transferring soon, but a lot of the students were at least three years younger than me. I was thinking, "Okay, I need to take this class and get out. I need to get my classes done so I can go and transfer to where I want to go. Get my B.A. And be done." Because the same way I had a circle of friends that were stuck here, I had a circle of friends who were already in grad school, already married, who were already in their careers.

I felt like I was stuck in limbo because I was in between these circles of friends. To me, I see them and I need to get to where they're at. Then I look at the other side. I don't want to be there.

I told myself, "Okay, I'm four years behind my peers but I wasn't at home. I wasn't stuck in community college for four years. I was doing something else." I didn't take the traditional path to college so that makes me feel a little bit better, but at the same time I know I don't have any time to waste. Time's ticking. I'm getting older. I have dreams and aspirations to get my master's. To get my Ph.D. I know I need to be on the fast track.

I don't have to limit myself. I can go anywhere.

I remember the first time I met Karen, my counselor. She was the counselor for me at the Veteran's Services Office, where I was employed. I came in and I knew I wanted to transfer. I was thinking, "I'll go to community college first and then I'll transfer to Cal State Fullerton." I remember I sat down with her for the first time when I was getting ready to start spring of '07. She was like, "What are your plans? What do you want to do?" I was like, "Well, I want to be here for two years. Then I want to transfer to Cal State Fullerton." And she's like, "Why are you going to transfer to Cal State Fullerton?" And I was like, "Because it's close." And then she's like, "What are you interested in doing?" And at that time, I knew I wanted to do something in communications. And she's like, "Have you looked at other schools?" And I was like, "No." And she was like, "Why don't you look into this or that place?" I know she mentioned a couple of UC's. Then she said USC. I was like, "Oh, I've always wanted to go there! I've always heard about it." Then she was like, "You know, just because you come to this community college, it doesn't mean you have to go to Cal State Fullerton." And in my mind, I knew it, but hearing her say it, I knew she was right. I don't have to limit myself. I can go anywhere.

That was the moment it hit me. I don't have to settle! A lot of people, they have their own reasons for why they go down the street. Some people have different situations. Whatever their reasons may be. But to me, if I did go to Cal State Fullerton, then I was settling. I didn't want to settle. I had to sacrifice! I have sacrificed so much to get to where I am now that I was like, "No. I'm not going to limit myself. I'm going to apply and go anywhere I want." So I think that was the moment when I was like, "Yeah. I'm going to go to school. I'm going to go to where I want to go."

As I did the research, first I thought the stereotypical, "Oh, you have to have money or someone in your family had to go there first, like your mom, your dad, or your great grandpa." Everybody else always says you can't get in. After I talked to Karen, I went home. I did the research. I looked at the statistics. I was like, "I can get in!" A lot of people I knew were like, "Where do you want to go to school?" I was like, "I want to go to a UC." They were like, "No, really, where do you want to go?" People that I was taking classes with at the community college said that. A lot of people fit that stereotype. They don't know any better. I was like, "How do you know I can't get in there? How do you know YOU can't get in there? You'll never know unless you try or you apply. The worst they can say is no. But at the same time, you shouldn't put all your eggs in one basket. You should try other places too. Apply to other places." So, to me, I knew that if I was able to get in there, then everything I was going to go through and put myself through while being here was going to be worth it.

To plan to transfer out, I knew meeting with the counselor was essential. I knew keeping the same counselor would be best. The entire time I was at community college, Karen was the only counselor that I would talk to.

To plan to transfer out, I knew meeting with the counselor was essential. I knew keeping the same counselor would be best. The entire time I was at community college, Karen was the only counselor that I would talk to. Sometimes she'd be busy. She wasn't the Veteran's counselor at a certain point. There was somebody else. The staff person was like, "There isn't a wait to meet with this other counselor." And I was like, "No, that's okay." I knew it was going to be a little bit harder when Karen moved from the Veteran's Services Office, even though she was only across the street. I was like, "No, I can wait the two weeks to talk to her." She was really responsive via email too, she was easily accessible. And if I had a die-hard question, she would always get back to me. And that was important because I had heard through peers like, "Oh, my counselor doesn't know anything" or "I met with somebody else last time and now this week I'm meeting with somebody else." That inconsistency would hold people back because you're listening to different people tell you different things. You have to be consistent with who you go to for advice. She was the only one I would talk to. It was always good.

When it came time to apply, a lot of the universities I applied to were because of my major. All the ones that I applied to fit my major because that's what I had heard. It was one of the things that Karen had told me. She's like, "Apply to the best school that suits your needs and what you want to get out of it." She's like, "Don't not apply to certain schools because you're afraid you're not going to get in or because you don't think you have the money to pay for it." She's like, "You need to go where you are going to get the most out of it in what you're trying to attain."

I applied to UC Santa Cruz. I applied to Cal State San Diego but I thought Cal State San Diego was a private Cal State University for some reason. USC because I had already lived far away from home and I was like, "I need to be in traveling

distance where I can still come and see my family on a Sunday."
I wanted to be close to them, but maybe not with them. Like
down the street, not in the same house. I wanted to have that
college experience that everyone always talks about. Living at
home I wouldn't be able to get that college experience, which is
why I always tell my sisters, "You can leave mom. She's going
to be okay. You don't have to go far away but you can distance
yourself from her."

My family was super supportive.
A lot of the times I wanted to give up. I didn't because of them.
Because I couldn't let them down.

   Still, it was hard. I don't think it was hard for my family
because they were used to me being away, especially since I was
in the military. I was always two hours away or on the other side
of the world. My mom knew that. She said, "Whatever it takes,
apply wherever you want to go." They're really supportive. My
family was super supportive. A lot of the times I wanted to give
up. I didn't because of them. Because I couldn't let them down.
My mom has always been there for me, since I started
community college, "I know you're going to get there. You're
going to go somewhere else. I'm really proud of you." Her
constant support is one of the things that kept me going. Like
when the tough gets going. I'm like, "No, no, no, I have to do
this. Primarily for myself but also for my family." And then
friendship-wise and socially, it was hard because I went through
it by myself. I had to do the application process by myself. I
would talk to the girls, Belleise and Yaz, and they'd be like, "I
don't know. What are you doing next year? You let us know how
it goes." So to me that was hard.
   I had to face transferring head on by myself. I did a lot of
research. I went on the internet. I did the CSU application way
in advance. I knew the CSU, UC deadlines way in advance. I

asked questions because they have two separate deadlines. I was confused. I was always in here talking to John in the Transfer Center. I was like, "Do I have to do this?" And he's like, "No." "Do I have to do this?" He's like, "Yeah." And then he's like, "Then this happens." He was a big help because I had nobody else to go to. All my friends from high school went from high school to college. They were like, "Yeah, I didn't do that. I wish I could help you but I don't really know or it was such a long time ago that I don't even remember." They couldn't relate. Then my current friends couldn't relate. So I was like, "Alright I can do this." Yeah, it was hard because I didn't want to leave my friends who were transferring the following year. I knew that they were all going to experience it together so I felt left out.

I even told John, "What happens if I wait?" He's like, "YOU'RE NOT WAITING! If I have to kick you out myself, you're going!" Then I was like, "It was just a thought!" We would kid around. Yaz and Belleise would say, "You should just stay." "I should, huh?" Then I would think to myself, "No holding myself back. I need to get me to where I want to go." I knew that our friendships were strong enough. The bonds that we had built were strong enough that regardless of whether I was here or I was there, we would still remain friends. And we have remained friends. Now that everybody's going their separate ways, it's eerie because they're like, "Now we know what you went through. Now we know why it was such a big deal when you wanted to get out." Now they see it. I'm like, "See! I told you."

I was admitted to my first choice, which is 'SC. My second choice was UC Santa Barbara. I was admitted there too. And then, I applied to UCLA. That was on a whim. I didn't really want to go there. I knew that I hadn't taken the right classes to get in there so when they said that I wasn't admitted, I knew it would happen that way. Then I applied to San Diego State. I didn't get in. I applied to UC San Diego. I got in. Then I applied to Cal State LA and Cal State Fullerton. I got in to both. So I knew that I had options and then 'SC was the last one.

I immediately had that positive attitude but as the wait got longer and longer, my self-doubt started getting bigger and bigger. What if I don't get in? What if they don't accept me? What if I can't afford it? What am I going to do?

At first, I committed to UC Santa Barbara. I completed the Statement of Intent to Register and everything. I talked to John in the Transfer Center. I was like, "'SC doesn't let us know til after the SIR May 1st deadlines. If I don't commit anywhere, then I'm going to get stuck not going anywhere. What if I don't get in?" Early on when I was applying to 'SC, I was like, "I'm going to get in. I know I'm going to get in." I immediately had that positive attitude but as the wait got longer and longer, my self-doubt started getting bigger and bigger. What if I don't get in? What if they don't accept me? What if I can't afford it? What am I going to do? John was the person that I would come talk to. I was like, "What do I do?" He's like, "You still haven't heard from them?" I was like, "No." He's like, "Use your backup Cal State and your backup UC." He's like, "All you have to do is send in the SIR. Afterward, if you do get in to USC, then you can say that you're withdrawing. That you decided against going." I was like, "You can do that?" He's like, "Yeah." I was like, "Okay!" So I committed to Santa Barbara. I told them that I would be going there.

Since the first time I talked to Karen two years ago, 'SC was the goal. At the same time, I knew that I couldn't put all my eggs in one basket. I made sure that I followed both the IGETC and the USC general education transfer requirements, which are two completely different transfer plans. The way I tackled it and chose my classes was, I took the classes that would comprise both of the requirements for both of those. All of those classes, I had to do. So 'SC was that, "AHH! If I got in, then all the sacrifice and all my goals would be accomplished! The reason why I came to community college, my two years. I'd be done!"

When I got the acceptance notice from USC,
it was the greatest feeling ever! I jumped up and down!
I gave myself an asthma attack! It was really good!

When I got the acceptance notice from USC, it was the greatest feeling ever! I jumped up and down! I gave myself an asthma attack! It was really good! I felt like I really accomplished something. At first, I had no financial aid package from USC. All I had was my acceptance letter. All they said was, "You're admitted."

Little did I know from doing my research, I overlooked the supplemental financial aid part of the application for USC. I thought all I had to do was the FAFSA, but 'SC requires you to send in all this other stuff, like the copies of your tax forms and then you have to do this other CSS profile on collegeboard.com. Lourdes in the Financial Aid Office told me about it. It was during graduation. I had term papers. It escaped my mind. Now that I know better, it's one of the first things I do. That's what delayed my financial aid package because they didn't have all my information.

Even so, I decided on USC. Everybody was like, "If they accepted you, that's a big thing. They're going to work with you. They're going to do whatever it takes to get you there." Then once I got accepted, I took a personal campus tour. I visited the offices. I was like, "I still don't know what my financial aid package looks like." The USC lady said, "Don't worry about it. That should be the least of your worries. They'll get you here." That made me feel better.

Once I got in is when I took the initiative to go and tour the school. I was like, "I was just accepted, what do I need to do?"

People were really helpful, which is really surprising because of that stereotype. I'm coming all alone. Nobody in my family has been there before. We don't have any money. I cannot afford it by myself. So I was afraid but soon I learned that everybody is in the same boat as I am, I didn't feel so alone anymore.

Going through the transfer process is very motivating. It makes you feel empowered. I don't think I would have the appreciation I have for my education had I not lived the transfer experience. I really don't think so because it makes you value what you have. It makes you value the opportunities that are allotted to you. You're basically the person that you make or you aren't. You are the only person that's going to define that. You are the one who is going to decide that. My life is in my hands literally. If I don't succeed, if I don't do it for myself, nobody else is going to do it for me. That's why I feel very empowered. I appreciate my life very much. I don't think I would be the person that I am today had I not lived the transfer experience. I really don't.

The best thing I ever did was not conforming. Not falling into the stereotypes or the expectations. Everybody was like, "Oh, you're probably going to do cosmetology." I'm like, "No, I don't want to do cosmetology." I mean no offense to the people who do. If that works for you, that works for you. A lot of people, they hear you or they see you. They're like, "Oh, where do you go to school?" At first, I'd be like, "I go to community college." And they'd be like, "Oh, so how long have you been there?" I'm like, "A year." And they'd be like, "So, what do you want to do?" I was like, "I'm going to transfer." "Really?" "Yes, that's the purpose of a community college! That's why you go to a community college because you're going to transfer somewhere." Breaking that stereotype is one of my proudest moments.

You're basically the person that you make or you aren't.
You are the only person that's going to define that.
You are the one who is going to decide that. My life is in my
hands literally. If I don't succeed, if I don't do it for myself,
nobody else is going to do it for me.

To be a success, you need to find or make a network of support. You need self-motivation. You need self-discipline. That's one of the biggest ones. You need the right peers. You need to be open to anything. You have to be willing to try things and to be open to what the results are going to be. And also, know that it's not going to be easy. Especially at a community college, you can be easily sucked in. You have to be your own driving force and work really hard.

A good student support program should have not only peers mentors but professional mentors, Latina women who have lived the experience and have come out on the end as very successful. It needs to be very diverse. Oftentimes when people think of Latina women, they think everyone wants to be a teacher. That's not always the case. Mentors need to be not only educationally diverse but they also need to be culturally diverse because there're a lot of women that are successful and have families. Also, there are a lot of women who are successful and don't have families. Within our own community, there needs to be a bigger exposure to diversity. Everyone thinks of a Latina, it's the same one. But, no, there are so many!

Another thing that should be a part of a program is counseling services because everyone has different experiences and has experienced a different walk in life. That can be a little bit hard sometimes.

Students also need to know that they shouldn't be afraid to
speak up. Don't be afraid to ask questions.

Students also need to know that they shouldn't be afraid to speak up. Don't be afraid to ask questions. Don't fall into norms. Don't be a statistic.

If I did my transfer experience all over again, I probably would've studied more my final semester. I did study enough, but I probably would've studied even more. Because my last semester, I don't think I did as well as I could've done. A lot of that had to do with the fact that I was on my own at the time all the applications were due. I was busy hearing back from the schools and preparing, making my transfer plans. The accumulation of all of that, plus taking 18 units was too much. I knew that I was going to pass all my classes, failure was not an option. I figured as long as I got a B, I was going to be okay. That's never been my mentality ever. But I was like, "It's okay, as long as I get a B, I'll be fine." I settled.

I knew that it wasn't going to harm me. I was like, "No, I'll still get admitted as long as I pass the class. I'll still get into the colleges I want." But for myself, knowing that I gave it my all my last semester would have been something that I could have been even more proud of. But that's because I'm my own biggest critic. A lot of people would be like, "Well, you still graduated with honors." And I was like, "Yeah, I did. But deep down inside, I know that I could have done better."

Latinas look at other college students or the majority of college students but the college students don't look like them. Then they think that they can't do it because the success stories are so few. It's hard. I see it where 65% of the student population's Caucasian. I'm like, "You don't look like me. You don't talk like I do. You don't come from where I come from." So, of course, if I'm somebody on the outside looking in, you can get easily discouraged. At the same time, you have to look for that community. It's there. You have to go and find it. Then feel like, "Oh, here's where everybody else looks like me. They're making it happen so I can make it work for me too." Often people only see what's on the outside. They conform. They don't really take a look at what's on the inside. Once they take a look at what's on the inside, then they would realize that there's a place for them in there too.

Too many people wait towards the end of the year. Then they are like, "Oh, so this is the Transfer Center." Like, "Where have you been all the year?" That's one of the things I experienced when I was on the Cheer Squad in community college. I would tell the girls, "How come you don't go on these campus tours? You just have to sign up at the Transfer Center." They would say, "There's a Transfer Center on campus?" It's because people are stuck in this commuter mentality. People think it's going to be spoon-fed to them. It's going to be given to them. It's like, "No! Is this what you want? You have to find it. You have to put in the work and the effort to go and get it. No one's going to give it to you." That's what's wrong with this society. I'd say, especially with the younger generation, everybody expects to be given stuff. That's not how it works.

Latinas in community college need to see that it's possible. For myself, I knew that that's what I wanted to do. That's the mentality that I came in with. A lot of people don't have a positive mentality. I see that with my sister. She's like, "Oh, that's you. I can't do it." Like, "Yes, you can! You can do it! My mom could do it, if she wanted to! Anybody can do it!" I don't know what it is that needs to be done or needs to be shown so that people can come in with the same positive mentality. When I hear my little sister say that, it breaks my heart! I'm constantly telling her, "No, you can do it too. You can do it." My sister says school comes easy to me or she complains that her counselor doesn't want to talk. Her counselor doesn't want to answer her questions. Community college students need to be like, "I PAY to go to school here. I'm not coming here for free or whatever. You're still getting paid. It's your job to listen to me. To guide me. To tell me what classes I need to take." If somebody's not doing that for you, then you need to find somebody that's gonna do it for you.

You're the one in control of your education.
If somebody's not going to help you get through it,
then they don't need to be in your plan or in your circle.

You're the one in control of your education. If somebody's not going to help you get through it, then they don't need to be in your plan or in your circle. It is so important to show people, it's possible. Especially to women, it's so possible! You can do it no matter if you have five kids, seven kids, it's all in your will and your want in yourself. You need to have the motivation and drive!

Profile update: Sapphire transferred to 'SC also known as the University of Southern California where she graduated with her Bachelor of Arts Degree as a double major in American Studies- Ethnicity and Spanish. She continued on to complete her Master Degree in Social Work also from the University of Southern California in May 2014. She is currently working with military veterans at the Veteran Affairs Department Outpatient Clinic in downtown Los Angeles.

Chapter Five
Go Get It, Mija, Go Get It!

I'm a first generation college student. Nobody else in my family has gone college. I remember in elementary school, in 6th grade, there were girls around me saying "I'm going to UCLA" or "I'm going to USC." I remember I didn't even know what those words meant.

I said, "I'm going to UCLA, too" because that was the cool thing to say, but I didn't even know where UCLA was, even though it was in Los Angeles. I had never been out of Orange County.

All I knew was that it was something you do after completing high school. That's all I knew. I didn't know the difference between community college, Cal State, UC, none of that. So I didn't really know what I was talking about at that point.

In high school, I thought about going to college,
but I mostly put it out of my head and avoided the
thought because I had really bad grades.

It made me feel like I was lacking something. Something that other students had at home. Conversations with parents or expectations that were placed on them that I didn't have. Maybe the ability to see beyond a certain point in the world. I didn't have that because no one ever talked to me about it. My parents said, not in elementary school but later on, like "Think about going to college. You should go to college." Especially my dad.

But never at that young of an age.

In high school, I thought about going to college, but I mostly put it out of my head and avoided the thought because I had really bad grades. I was motivated not so much by education but more as a way to get rid of the emotional stuff on my mind that was making me feel a lot of confusion. I wasn't focused on building that vision of my future at that age.

I remember before graduating high school I got really freaked out, because I was like, "Now what am I going to do?" I started thinking about community college. But that wasn't until after I graduated because my aunt said there was a job at the school that she could connect me with. That's when I first started envisioning myself in college.

After high school is when I started envisioning myself at a community college, at any kind of college.

I didn't know college was going to be as freeing as it was. I thought it would be another chance at high school. Where people throw work at you and you complete it. But this time I would be motivated so it would be different for me. I didn't know that there was that big of a difference between high school and college.

My aunt told me about a job at the community college. That's how I came to find out more about it. That's how I found out about EOPS. That's when I connected to an EOPS counselor. I started working in the EOPS Office. 'Cuz they said, "You're enrolling here, right?" I said, "Oh, yeah." I had planned to enroll but that gave me the extra push I needed to really be here full-time. Then they helped me to get the book award. They enrolled me in EOPS. It was a student hourly position in the EOPS Office.

With the job came this whole support system. The peer counselors, my academic counselor Joe Reyes, who is amazing! I had no idea that I would have this support system.

I was already thinking about coming to college but that was the push I needed to get me to really commit. To have a support system. It was almost like a gift. Here I heard about this job, then I said to myself "Ok, I'm gonna go apply." With the job came this whole support system. The peer counselors, my academic counselor Joe Reyes, who is amazing! I had no idea that I would have this support system. I wasn't very social then at that point. I was thinking, "Okay, I have to take control of my life." Now I've built relationships.

My family knew Joe, my counselor, was helping me, but I don't think they really grasped what was going on inside me that changed. There was a really big shift from me being a passive person to active person, creating the life that I wanted. That was the difference. That's what the support helped me do. It helped me to see myself, as a person that was shaping my own life.

There was a really big shift from me being a passive person to active person, creating the life that I wanted. That was the difference.

My dad would say, after I graduated from high school, "Go to college. Do everything you can. Whatever your goals are, go get it mija, go get it." He would always say that. He would bring me to school. He would tell me, even in high school he would tell me, "Professors don't like the people who sit in the back of the class. They like the people who sit in the front. The people that ask questions. The people that are resourceful." He would always be telling me that, but I was too lost in my emotional world to really listen. When I was in college, he would still tell me that. I finally took his advice but it didn't come directly from him so much. It came from me. It had to be internal. I started listening to my father. I started listening to my own voice too that was like, "You can do more than this. You are not 1.8 GPA

Dahlia, failing everything anymore."

I will never forget my first impression of community college. It was before I was taking classes. I came to campus to sign up for something. I was turning in something for my application. I was walking through the 100 building. There were all these classrooms. A counselor, Rolando Sanabria, was teaching a class in one of the classrooms. I was looking in through the doorway at the TV because he was playing a video by Les Brown for the class. He was playing the Les Brown video. He was talking about goals and finding your true potential. I was peering in and thinking, "Oh my god! This is what college is? This is awesome! This is just what I need!" Just then, the teacher came over to close the door. I was like, "Aaww…" But before I could finish that reaction, he said, "Do you want to come in and watch the rest of the video with the class?" And I was like, "Uh, okay." I was going to be entering a college classroom for the first time in my life. I was like, "Okay, sure." I walked in. I sat down. I finished watching the video. Then I said, "Thank you!" That was the most amazing moment ever! That's when I knew that people cared here. That was the difference. Then I left.

Then my aunt told me later that my grandpa actually coached Rolando when he was on the high school soccer team. And my grandpa passed away a long time ago when I was a little kid, like 5 years old. That was just an amazing moment! I knew I loved community college from the first moment I stepped foot on campus!

That was the most amazing moment ever! That's when I knew that people cared here. That was the difference.

I had a really positive experience planning my transfer process because I worked in EOPS. I also worked at other places on campus too. I worked at the Office of Special Programs, it is the office that houses the Honors Program. My second semester, that's when I found out about the Honors Program. I applied to join. I found out that your chances of transferring to a place you wanna go to go up if you are in the Honors Program. Especially for UCLA, there was something like a 94% acceptance rate for Honors students with a certain GPA. That seemed awesome! I knew the program would help me reach my goal.

I graduated from high school with a 1.8 GPA. My first semester in community college, I had a 3.55 GPA but I knew some of those classes were non-transferable. I thought, "Okay, I'm gonna join this Honors Program." I knew that I could do better, that I needed a challenge. I knew I needed more difficult work. I needed work that would make me reflect more. I didn't need the "Memorize this" or whatever kind of work. I needed to be completely engaged in a classroom. That's what I was looking for. In high school I didn't have that. That is why I didn't do well. At community college, I wanted to get the most out of school.

What really helped me was one time I went to talk to my academic counselor, Joe Reyes. I told him, "Joe, I want to do the least I can 'cuz I know I'm not that smart. I want to transfer anywhere. The place that has the least amount of requirements. That's where I wanna go." He said "What are you talking about? Your scores on your assessment tests show that you can do so much better." He said that I could go to a UC or something. I was like, "Whatever, ha-ha, yeah, right!" I didn't really believe him at that point. The thing was that he saw what I didn't see. That's why I stuck to him like glue, because that was so nurturing for me. It fed my spirit and helped me to keep moving toward my goal when I might not have had the motivation on my own. All of the energy and all the drive I needed, he helped me to build that inside of myself. I knew that he knew what he was talking about. He was like a father figure to me. Like the way my dad would have been if my dad had been educated.

I knew that I could do better, that I needed a challenge.
I knew I needed more difficult work.
I needed work that would make me reflect more.
I didn't need the "Memorize this" or whatever kind of work.
I needed to be completely engaged in a classroom.

My dad had a 2nd grade education. He would see something in me and he wanted it to be true. He never finished school. He always said he felt bad because he did not go to school. He wanted me to be his first daughter to achieve the goal that he could never achieve but he didn't know how to tell me how to do it.

I didn't find out about his lack of education until later. My father was gone a lot because he is a truck driver, so he wasn't there very often. He was the motivating force behind me trying hard in school. When he would leave, I didn't really have a reason to try anymore. He would tell me. "Go to college" and "Education is so important." One time I was in the car with him. I was failing all my classes in junior high. Or a lot of 'em. One time, he told me crying that his dad took him out of school in 2nd grade. His father would beat him because at school he would get beaten up and his lunch money would get taken away, so he had to go work with his dad in the sugarcane farm in Guatemala.

It's not like I didn't care, it's just that I wasn't ready in junior high and high school. There was too much chaos. I couldn't grab onto that as anything that would motivate me.

Once I started to achieve good grades and work in
different offices at the community college,
then I started to feel like I could achieve.

Once I started to achieve good grades and work in different offices at the community college, then I started to feel like I could achieve. That I could make him proud, then it was like, "Yay, I can do this! I can make him proud of me in that way. The way he really wanted me to."

I joined the Honors Program. It didn't really help me understand, it just helped me know that if I kept on this route, then I would pretty much get in somewhere. Somewhere decent, at least in my opinion.

Being in the Honors Program allowed me to understand what it was to be a college student. A real college student. Not a high school student who is going to college, not someone that came from high school and is now in college, but an actual college student. I started to understand I am supposed to bring my experience into the classroom. That's what it's all about. That's where I am really good because I am so reflective. I took Philosophy my second semester. I took Philosophy 100 Honors and I took History 170 Honors. I don't know how I did that because I was still feeling like I was not smart. I believed I couldn't learn. I was in the Honors classes thinking to myself, "I can't learn. What am I doing here? I am not smart. What am I doing here with all these people that are obviously smarter than I am?" I struggled so much with those thoughts in my head.

In my classes I learned to digest a lot of information. Then be able to present it to the class in an intelligent way. To not let my fear get in the way of what I had to do. That is a major part of the transfer and the college choice process.

The thing with the Honors Program is that you have to work in groups or you have a partner when you do assignments. Then I would talk to people about the class. I didn't just stay quiet. I was like, "Oh my gosh, I'm so incompetent." I would actually tell this girl that this was how I felt. She would say, "No, all you have to do is do the work. Don't think like that."

I was also reading self-help books at the time. I started doing positive affirmations. I started writing on my mirror with lipstick, positive affirmations. I would repeat them to myself every day. I did a lot of personal reflection at the same time I was taking classes.

I remember one time being in the EOPS Office. I didn't know that they did progress reports. I was sitting with Andre Strong. He was my peer counselor. He said, "Oh, I got your progress report." Then I said "Yeah?" and he said, "It looks really good." And it was from Ms. Mettleship. She was so funny! She would dress up in costumes! One time she was Ms. Addams and stayed in character the whole class period. That was part of it too. The class really appealed to my sense of imagination. So many parts of it, the Honors classes challenged me but it was also more fun. Anyway, Andre took out my progress report. My professor said that I was one of the brightest students in class. That I was doing really good work or amazing work or something like that.

That someone like her, she was from the east coast.
She had a Ph.D. in History. That someone like her could
look at someone like me, from a poor area of town and from
apartments where I shared a room with my two sisters and
almost didn't graduate from high school, and she is saying
that I'm one of the brightest students in the class.
That was a really big compliment!

That conversation was like a slap in the face! I thought, "Dahlia, you are smart! Stop feeling like you can't learn!" That someone like her, she was from the east coast. She had a Ph.D. in History. That someone like her could look at someone like me, from a poor area of town and from apartments where I shared a room with my two sisters and almost didn't graduate from high school. She is saying that I'm one of the brightest students in the class. That was a really big compliment! That was a really proud day for me.

When it was time to complete my college applications, I applied to UC Santa Barbara, UC San Diego, UC Davis, and UCLA.

I didn't apply to Cal States because Joe told me that I could go to the UCs. I knew that with the Honors Program I could do it. I could get into a UC because I had good grades. I didn't wanna go anywhere else but the UC.

There was one mistake I made. Through the Honors Program I had a chance to get scholarships but I didn't apply to any private schools. I didn't know a lot about private universities. It was a mistake because my experience would have been better at a liberal arts school. Considering my personality, it would have been a better fit for me. Like Whittier College or Pomona College, or something like that. I saw the well-known names and the reputation. At the same time I feel I should have researched more. As self-directed as I was at that point, I should have been more open. But all you ever hear about is UCLA, UC Santa Barbara, UC this, UC that. There should be more of a presence of private schools at community colleges. I should have researched further, because I didn't know that an atmosphere like that could really exist for me. I didn't know how financial aid could fund a private university education. I'd heard it was so much more expensive.

As far as out-of-state universities, there was never a thought in my mind that I would go out of state. I heard all the best schools were here in California. Plus, I didn't want to go too far from my family 'cuz I didn't have a support system really outside of my immediate family. My extended family wasn't in my life at that point.

There should be more of a presence of private schools at community colleges. I should have researched further, because I didn't know that an atmosphere like that could really exist for me. I didn't know how financial aid could fund a private university education.

The application process was a very internal process for me. I

didn't really have a lot of people to talk to about it. The Transfer
Center completely influenced me because they took me on college tours. I remember one time we went on a northern California tour. We went to Cal States and UCs. That's the first time I
saw UC Santa Barbara. They catered the whole thing on the
beach. It was my dream school. I was like, "Oh my gosh, people
like me are walking around on this campus. This is the perfect
place. They have creative writing. There is an independent study
thing. This would be awesome!" Then Joe had gone to UCLA. I
knew that the name UCLA was important. I thought, "Oh that
might be cool." I was never actually serious about going to
UCLA. Never.

The only reason I applied to UCLA is because EOPS gave me
the application fee waiver for four UC campuses. My dream
school was UC Santa Barbara. I thought I could get in. Then I
visited. I thought it was a cool place to be. It was by the beach.
Then, San Diego. I wanted to go to San Diego. Then Davis. Because I remember they had a reality show on MTV. There was a
sorority at UC Davis so I was like, "Oh, okay. It looks like a nice
school, or whatever." I didn't really research the majors there. I
did the application really late, the last day that it was due. That's
when I turned it in. I worked on it all day. People should not do
this, but I stayed up all night writing my personal statement. No
one read it before I sent it off to the four schools. So wrong!

I already applied to the schools that I wanted to apply to, the
three, but I had one more left because of the application fee
waiver. Berkeley. I don't know. I probably won't get in. UCLA,
well, I probably still won't get into UCLA but at least it's better
than completely throwing it away and applying to UC Berkeley
'cuz I probably won't get in there. So whatever, I'll apply to
UCLA. My last choice. My complete shot-in-the-dark yeah-right,
never-gonna-happen choice. I just needed one more school to
fill this out so I could send in my application.

Turns out, I was accepted at all the schools I applied to! My first choice was Santa Barbara. My second choice would have been San Diego. My third choice would have been Davis. And then I didn't even count UCLA as a choice.

I remember I had my Statement of Intent to Register and my deposit in an envelope on top of the TV. I told my sister to tell my dad to take it to the post office. It was to hold my spot at Santa Barbara. Then a couple days later or something, I got an e-mail from UCLA that I was accepted 'cuz they do it the latest. I was like, 'Nooo!' I ran to get the envelope from on top of the TV. I ripped that envelope right up!

What happened was that I was so in awe of the fact that UCLA would want me that it made me feel smart. Worthy. Amazing. I actually went beyond the goal that I set for myself. Coming from a 1.8 GPA in high school. Going to a UC was already the most amazing thing that I could've ever envisioned, but going to someplace where so many people wanna go? Not just for first generation college students but everybody in the world and their mom.

My dad was actually the deciding factor. I said, "Dad, I got into Santa Barbara. It's the school where I really wanna go, but I got into UCLA too." He's all, "Well, what's the difference?" I said, "UCLA's way harder." He said, "When have you ever done anything because it was easy?"

My dad was actually the deciding factor. I said, "Dad, I got into Santa Barbara. It's the school where I really wanna go, but I got into UCLA too." He's all, "Well, what's the difference?" I said, "UCLA's way harder." He said, "When have you ever done anything because it was easy?"

During that time my dad told me that he had a brain tumor. I watched my dad get out of bed and go to work even though he had a brain tumor. He would be so happy that he had a load to take, because he was a truck driver. He was my role model.

He can't be obviously in his education but with his work ethic.
As strong as he is. That he could still get joy from work even
though he knew he had a brain tumor and he could die.

As an adult, I had to deal with a lot of hard things emotionally. But I didn't let it affect me in my education. When I got to
community college, I changed my mind. I completely changed
and he saw me change.

*When I got in and I got the acceptance e-mail, I started
screaming. I ran out to the living room. My parents were
watching soccer. I was like, 'I got in! I got in!'
I was screaming really loud and jumping up and down.
My mom was happy and my dad was stunned.*

My dad didn't really understand what UCLA meant as a university. When I got in and I got the acceptance e-mail, I started
screaming. I ran out to the living room. My parents were watching soccer. I was like, 'I got in! I got in!' I was screaming really
loud and jumping up and down. My mom was happy and my
dad was stunned. They were like "Oh good mija, good job. Good
for you." And then later, they told me all they saw when I was
yelling were dollar signs.

It was so crushing. They told that to me a good while later.
They were like 'Oh, that's grrrrreat...' but really they were thinking, "Crap, how are we going to afford that?"

But the way that I've experienced being how I am in life is
that I don't let reality get me down. I always live in the possibil-
ities. I didn't care how I was gonna afford to do it, I was gonna
go to UCLA!

My aunt spilled the beans to my counselor, Joe, because she
has a really big mouth. I love my aunt but she has a really big
mouth. They were working in the same office actually. He said
he was so proud! He didn't know I was gonna do that. Not that
he did not believe in me or anything. More like, "Oh my gosh,

she came in here saying I'm not smart. I have a 1.8 GPA. Then she gets herself admitted to the same school that I went to?" Joe was from East LA but he went to Catholic school. He learned Latin. He's super smart. Then I'm like "Yeah, I'm going to UCLA too."

The transfer process, as a student, made me realize I always wait until the last minute. Obviously because I'm a procrastinator. I've always been a procrastinator. I have a support system at the community college. I was here at the Transfer Center all the time. Someone was always asking like, "Have you applied?" but I didn't listen. I was like, "Yeah yeah yeah I'll do it later." I went through everything so fast! I had already completed all my classes. In two and a half years, I did everything plus the Honors Program, plus I worked, plus I was involved in everything. That means that the November before that I was applying, in a year and a half, I was already applying! I had just graduated from high school with a 1.8 GPA the year before. I couldn't wrap my head around how that was happening so fast. In so little time I could turn it around completely. Completely be a different person. It made me feel like anything was possible when I got accepted... like anything! As long as I was willing to work hard for it.

That means that the November before that I was applying, in a year and a half, I was already applying! I had just graduated from high school with a 1.8 GPA the year before. I couldn't wrap my head around how that was happening so fast. In so little time I could turn it around completely. Completely be a different person. It made me feel like anything was possible when I got accepted... like anything! As long as I was willing to work hard for it.

The transfer process doesn't erase my previous life path but I was now drawing a new life path. My future life is newly blank. It feels like now I am imagining and creating the next phase in my life. A new road is rolling out. There are these different landscapes like, "Oh, wow!" And it's so different from what I was living before. Somehow I always knew inside of me that there was something like this out there for me. That's why I didn't stop. That's why I joined the Honors Program and everything. Even though I had really low self-esteem from the achievements that I hadn't had yet or hadn't completed yet, I built up my confidence. I knew I could do it. I'd gotten accepted. Of course, there was still fear, like I don't know if I was gonna be good enough.

Somehow I felt like I went too far! "Why did I apply? Now that I'm accepted, am I gonna be able to be that UCLA student? And graduate?" It's always been easy for me to get in. Every job I ever applied for. This other program I'm in now. It's actually being there and doing all the work that's hard for me. Not setting up this picture of myself to let myself or everyone else down but to live up to the expectations. Live up to this picture that I've painted of myself. Of whom I could be.

When I was graduating from high school, I remember something inside of me was like, "Oh, hell no, you deserve better than this." It was the summer after high school. I worked someplace where I experienced racism and prejudice. I knew that I deserved respect. That the only way that I was going to get that was to properly educate myself. Follow through on my potential. 'Cuz if I could do that, then no one could put me down because I know that I'm where I am supposed to be.

In that moment where I experienced racism and prejudice, not only did I feel like a failure but I was perceived as that. I couldn't respond when someone called me a failure. Or stupid or whatever. I couldn't say "No, I'm not." One of the women at work brought in her high school yearbook and showed me how she was as a cheerleader in high school. That was so many years-like 20 years ago. Or 15. I was like, "I'm not gonna be her. I'm not gonna let the best times of my life be in high school."

I also found motivation from my sisters. Being a role model for my sisters. Giving my parents something to be proud of...

I also found motivation from my sisters. Being a role model for my sisters. Giving my parents something to be proud of because at work my mom would hear comments, or she would talk about how other people's children were doing this or that. She never had anything to talk about for me. Once I went to school, she had something to say now. My parents, they've been really stuck for a while. Financially. They didn't really have anything to be proud of for themselves.

Now they tell me stories about work. My dad, he didn't really get what was up with UCLA. I gave him a UCLA baseball hat. He wore it while he was driving to Texas and back. That was his route. The people at the gas stations would stop him. They would say, "Who's going to UCLA? Your daughter?" And he would say "Yes," and they would say, "You know, that's a really good school!" or something like that, and he would feel so proud. But he didn't know it was a really good school. He didn't know anything about it.

For me to be successful at transferring from the community college, I needed to have a support system. That was a big component of it. The staff in the Transfer Center and my counselor. I really depended on faculty and staff. And the students, sure I had friends and acquaintances but they didn't go with me when I transferred. If I would have depended on them, then I would have settled for whatever they were doing. To do what they were doing. I wanted to see what people that had been through it saw in me. To see that I could do it. Not people that were at the same level. Being in their company, I realized I could do that. I can do that too. Not just achieve, but maybe have a career like that.

I transferred when I was 21. When I was 20, before I transferred, they interviewed me at the community college about what career I wanted. I said that I wanted to be a college counselor.

To be successful, you need information and support, having someone nagging you to remember, and to do whatever you need to do. That's what the Transfer Center provides. There are people there. You need people that are nagging you and all the dates and all the information. I'm not really that detail-oriented. I have a lot of things going on in my head all the time. It's really important to have that place. The people that will remind you not only that you can do it, but that you need to do it now. Now!

Just as important is having access to challenging academic courses at the community college level that are comparable to what's at a UC. Plus, having the option to join the Honors Program. The high school classes are so low. Once you take AP classes, that's how a normal high school class should be. I'm from a low-income area where the parents aren't fighting to get more advanced classes, the high school teachers don't always see the potential in the students.

My family is probably the most important part of being the type of person that would actually complete the transfer process.

It is so important to have challenging classes. Challenging material. Even if parents don't tell you how, just the fact that they think you can do it is so important.

Something that helped me is having the example of being a hard worker. Both of my parents are really hard workers.

As far as being a success in college, I don't always value everything my family has done for me. I lacked the knowledge of how to go to college and how to actually transfer and everything, but my family is probably the most important part of being the type of person that would actually complete the transfer process.

Without my family, I wouldn't have been able to transfer. I wouldn't have had, not only the money, but the emotional support. When you leave everything behind, all you have is that call to your family. "Come and pick me up this weekend so we can hang out." Before you've made friends, before you've done all that. You make the decision and it's like, "Now what?" All you have from your past, really, is your family. To keep you connected to who you are and everything because of your values.

You go to a different campus and values are so different. UCLA and the community college, the values are completely different. At the community college, the human connection is important and people see you as a whole student. When you go to a place like UCLA, you are this person coming in to do work. Everyone's very competitive. A lot of it is about image. The people that I was around are no longer like me. The only people I could express myself with or talk to about that was my family. That was it.

If I could go back and change anything about how I transferred, I would have applied for more scholarships. I de-selected myself from opportunities like scholarships. I de-selected myself from UCLA but I clicked the button anyway. I wasn't going to and my life would have been completely different right now. UCLA was more challenging and maybe I should have gone to Santa Barbara. It would have been a great time. Maybe I would be a writer right now.

I really enjoy my life right now because there's a lot of growth. When I went to UCLA, I realized the challenges that students face and that I needed to help.

I say, don't de-select yourself. Let them reject you, don't reject yourself. Don't reject yourself for them, whether it's a scholarship or a school!

I say, don't de-select yourself. Let them reject you. Don't reject yourself. Don't reject yourself for them, whether it's a scholarship or a school!

The most important ingredient to success is understanding that you have a choice in your life. Every moment, every choice you make, you're creating what your future is gonna be. Because it can all turn around in a year and a half!

Profile update: Dahlia transferred to the University of California, Los Angeles and graduated with her Bachelor of Arts Degree in English - American Literature and Culture. Dahlia continued her education and graduated with her Master of Science Degree in Counseling - Student Development in Higher Education at Long Beach State University. She is currently working as an educational counselor helping students in the college choice process.

Chapter Six

It's so Mexican!

I always knew I was going to go to college. My brother and my sister went to college, So, I was next in line. It wasn't even a question of mine. On my mother's side of the family, everyone went to college. But on my father's, it's not so much expected. I'm closer to my mother's side, so you tend to follow who you're closer to. I knew I was going to go to college. I didn't know where but I knew it had to be somewhere local.

It wasn't like, "Let's go straight to the boring university." It was my choice. "Where do you want to go? JC or four-year university?" I wasn't very confident. My friends and I, a group of us said, "We should all go to community college. Go to the JC." Then we wanted to transfer over. I wasn't sure what I wanted my major to be, so I didn't want to waste my time. I knew that I had to take remedial classes so I came straight to the community college instead of going to the four-year university. I didn't feel prepared. I didn't feel motivated very much either. I was scared and very nervous. It wasn't that community college was the easier route but it was a little spaced out, a little bit more than going straight to the four-year university. I felt that I was going to do the same kind of classes at the university that I could do over there. I wanted to start at the community college, take a couple of classes, and then choose my major from there.

I felt scared of the idea of going straight to a four-year. I didn't feel like the high school had prepared me very well for college classes. They had a lot of workshops for financial aid and stuff. I don't think that the school prepared me on what it really was to be on your own and to know how to be self-motivated to finish things on your own.

I felt scared of the idea of going straight to a four-year. I didn't feel like the high school had prepared me very well for college classes. They had a lot of workshops for financial aid and stuff. I don't think that the school prepared me on what it really was to be on your own and to know how to be self-motivated to finish things on your own.

My siblings both went to trade schools. Then my cousin went straight to a four-year university, so I was the first one to go to a community college. Nobody was there to tell me "This is how it is. This is how it's going to be for you. Take these types of classes."

My core group of friends, we helped each other out. "Oh, did you hear we have to go take the placement test? Okay, when? You call. Okay then let's go together." I didn't have anybody to show me, "These are the steps that you have to take before you go."

Our senior year of high school, my friends and I decided together to go to community college. The four-year university was already out of sight. We hadn't talked about it really. It was something that we never really talked about. Most of us wanted to do the "girlier" stuff: be a fashion designer or do cosmetology. No one ever said a lawyer or doctor. Nothing like that. We only talked about college towards the last year of high school. I considered it but I wasn't thinking, "Okay, what university do I want to attend my freshmen year?" It wasn't said and my parents didn't ask.

*We only talked about college towards the last year of
high school. I considered it but I wasn't thinking, "Okay,
what university do I want to attend my freshmen year?"
It wasn't said and my parents didn't ask.*

Originally I thought I was going to go to a trade school, like
Devry University. That's what my brother did. I thought I was
going to do something like that. The two year program and get
into the work force, but thank God I didn't go that route.

When I decided to attend community college, I didn't talk so
much to my cousins or my sister about that as much as I did with
my brother. I was closer to my brother than I was with my sister.
My brother's the oldest. I was like, "I don't want to do that. I'm
not sure what I want to do yet. I want to get my Associate's,
right? And transfer?" He was always very supportive of me. I
never really talked to anybody else about college.

As far as my cousins, they did go to college. But none of my
aunts or uncles went to college. Luckily they all have really good
jobs. None of them have a university or college certificate. It's
just my cousins. They would ask me, "So you know where
you're going to go?" They didn't say, "This one has a great program or I've heard so much about this school." They didn't talk
about it like that. I don't know why. You don't really talk about
that in my family. It was more about, "What's going on with the
family?" and stuff or "Good to see you", or this or that person
asking you, "So, what do you want to be or what do you want
to do?" Then you just say, "Well, I'm going to go for my Associate's Degree. I'm going to go to community college and then
transfer over eventually. And what I have to do over there, I have
to do over here anyways so I'm just going to do it." My aunts
would ask me. On my other side, no one really asked.

Most of my father's side is still in Mexico so whenever we
would talk or see each other, it was really about catching up and
not so much, "So, what are you going to do now?" I do have my

cousins from my father's side, two of them who are lawyers and then my brother has his degree as well and my sister did massage therapy, which is a 2-year program. The rule in my house was "You're getting out of this house with some sort of degree or certificate." She went the shorter route. I saw her life. I thought this is exactly what I don't want. She got married at 20 years-old. She had her first child at 21 and her husband is way older. He's 6 years older than her. They're still together and everything. While it worked out for them, I knew that it wasn't what I wanted for myself.

Once my father asked me, "How do you imagine yourself going to work? Can you imagine yourself going in scrubs? Then maybe you want to be a nurse." And I was like, "No." I was like, "I want to be in heels. I knew I wanted to be in heels and in a work suit." I geared myself towards that. I didn't want to be in a store. Not that there's anything bad with that. Those are perfectly great jobs but I knew that I had envisioned myself in the long run how I really wanted to live my life. I don't want to be working at a factory and stuff like that so I knew that heels and suits were going to be my option. Working with my people. I love it. It's my passion now.

I have been working at my father's restaurant since when I was like 13 years old, 12-13 years old. I worked with him for many years. I would ask what everyone needed. I would take orders. I would fulfill whatever they wanted. I felt like that's something that I like. I like to work with people. I like to help them out in any way. If they speak Spanish then I'll speak Spanish and if English, then English. Any way that I could help. My family's like, "You have to be very polite." All of the values geared me towards listening to what my father asked of me.

In my senior year of high school, they asked me, "So what do you want to do? And make sure that this is what you want to do." They were supportive but they didn't ask me a lot. I got quiet support from my family about college. "I know you'll do this. I know you'll be fine." Maybe they saw that I was not that focused on school. Maybe they got a little worried but I think most of all I was a pretty good student. I was a cheerleader in high school. I was very involved in sports in my school so they knew that I had that drive.

When I first got to community college, I was very scared because I thought it was going to be like a foreign language to me. I don't think I came from high school to the college with the tools necessary for me to achieve at all. You had all these books and sometimes the professors would be like, "If you're not here, that's up to you, you're missing out." In high school, you have to go to all of your classes. They call your parents and would be like, "Why aren't you attending." But now it was based on self-motivation. Either you did it or did not. Most of all I believe that I was pretty self-motivated. I knew that I didn't have anyone to turn to besides my support group of friends. We were all going through it together. We would all take the same classes and then we would switch classes the next semester. We'd trade all our books. That is what we tried to do. My father didn't pay for anything for my college. He didn't pay for anything. Plus I never applied for financial aid. I never did that route, but my friends did. If one of them went to the office, she would phone the other one, "Once you do this, once you do that, then you take this." Being here with my other friends that attended at the same time, I have to thank them for everything.

> *Being here with my other friends that attended at*
> *the same time, I have to thank them for everything.*

One time in class, Janine, from the Career Center, spoke and she said, "I have this internship opportunity. I'm going to be interviewing." I went and I asked about it. She agreed to meet me. I got hired. I was working with her for a while. She told me that the Transfer Center had a position too. I was like, "Okay, I'm going to apply." I applied. A lot of people got interviews but I got hired. Then I was informed about the Transfer Center, about the Career/Life Planning Center. Those resources I then shared with my friends too. "Make sure you guys go see what kind of math you have to take because not all of us have to take the same math. Make sure you guys go. There is walk-in counseling." You have to take care of yourself. Nobody was at home telling me these are the classes that you have to take. Because nobody in my family did that. The JC route, the junior college route.

It wasn't until I finished English 60 and Math 40 that I started working at the Transfer Center and the Career and Life Planning Center. It was halfway towards my Associate's here.

When it came to filling out the college application, the Transfer Center totally helped me with that. I was helping other students fill out their applications before I knew how to apply for myself.

Working at the Transfer Center definitely helped me because I knew that sitting down, I was scared. I was very scared because it's either make it or break it. It's still going to take more time and more money so I better finish soon. I noticed everyone asks the same thing in here too. "Which units count to transfer? How do I calculate my GPA." We'd print out transcripts and we'd cross off everything that was under course number 100. We started going through it. I remember. I was very scared. As far as transferring, it was like, "Okay, here it goes! I've got nothing else to do here." My parents had asked me, "How much more time do you have in community college. When are you going to transfer?" I was with my cohort of my friends that transferred over. Unfortunately, some of us slipped through the cracks. There were only three of us that transferred over. We started out with seven of us. Only three of us made it.

I was with my cohort of my friends that transferred over.
Unfortunately, some of us slipped through the cracks.
There were only three of us that transferred over.
We started out with seven of us. Only three of us made it.

There was one friend who said, "I'm going to do cosmetology." She went a different route but she did start out to transfer. Another one got a full-time job. She's like, "I'm going to go to school part-time next semester" and she never re-applied. The other one would come to school and then drop classes. Then come back but always part-time. One class or two classes a semester. Then none.

I knew that that wasn't going to be one of my options. I knew that my parents supported me. I didn't have to pay for rent but for everything else, it was out of my pocket. They didn't help me with my first car. They didn't help me pay for anything, no insurance, no gas, no bills. Everything, all of the bills were mine but as far as school, they really felt like that would be too much to afford. My friend that needed to come part-time, she couldn't get financial aid. The one who decided to do cosmetology, well, she thought she was going to make a career out of it. It worked out for her for about a year. Then after that, not so much. For me, I felt like, this is what I want and this is how I'm going to do it. I didn't have to have a full-time job. Maybe she did to help around the house a little bit more but I didn't need it so I didn't consider having a full-time job. Just seeing them, I knew that way might work for them but I didn't have to go that route. Then I had my two other friends that were like, "Nope let's go, let's go." Seriously, support is what helped me. Otherwise it would have taken me longer. And working at the Transfer Center and working at the Career and Life Planning Center and taking courses with Rolando, "Oh my gosh!"

I took a class with him and that's when I decided that's what I want to do. I want to do Counseling. I want to do that. I was already working at the Transfer Center and at the Career and Life Planning Center too. I was like "This is what I want to do. I'm comfortable here, I like it."

I would also hear stories about Rolando, my counselor. He went to the same high school I did. He also had the same job and came to school here then transferred. I felt like if he could do it, I could do it. I felt like, it is possible. I saw people that did it who came from around the same area. He went to my high school and then he went to the same community college as me. I was like, "Okay, it is possible." Not just people that are from different places can do it. I can do it but with support, if I keep asking for help. I have to ask questions otherwise I'm not going to get anywhere. No one is going to tell me. Do this for you.

When it came time to choose where to apply, I met with my counselors. I met with Rolando here at the Transfer Center. Also my counselors helped me make sure I was taking the right classes for the university that I wanted to go to. I did see a couple that were like, Long Beach or Fullerton or Cal Poly but those were a drive. Those were a distance. I would hear very good recommendations about Human Services, which is what I wanted to pursue. I wanted to do Counseling. And then, after my cousin got married, her husband also did Human Services over there. He told me, "For counseling, well, you have to do Human Services. That's your major. That's what you need to do." I was like, "Okay, Human Services. Well, I'm going with that." And my other two friends, we all went to Cal State Fullerton. Everyone was close-knit to me. It helped me feel more comfortable.

I didn't want to do things by myself. I came here with friends. I wanted to leave with friends. But I wanted to keep going.

Then I started working for the city. I knew that that would look good on my resume. If I was to stay 3 or 4 months, you can't really put that on your resume. It doesn't really count. I wanted to stay with the city. They were very flexible and very happy about me going to school. The City Manager at the time also graduated from Cal State Fullerton. He would be like, "How's it going?" Also, the Deputy City Manager went to Cal State Fullerton, so they were very flexible. They knew that I wanted to stay with the city. If I went to Cal Poly Pomona or if I went to San Francisco or San Diego, then working at the city would be out of the picture. My two close friends would also be out of the picture so then I had to start all over again, a whole new life elsewhere. I don't think I was prepared for that. I don't know why, maybe I felt scared. I didn't want to do things by myself. I came here with friends. I wanted to leave with friends. But I wanted to keep going.

Luckily, all three of us graduated and a fourth friend was on the way, so there were 4 of us. Now I'm starting my senior year at the university. It's going to be me alone if I go to graduate school. That's it. I don't have the other 3 to go with me. But I already know what I want to do. I'm sure that that's what I want to do. I know. The other 3 don't want to do therapy. I want to do Marriage and Family Therapy. I know who to go to if I have questions. I know my advisers. They're very welcoming so I feel like, "Okay, I can do this." I can do this because I know that people will have my back.

Now my family does ask me, "How's school?" They see that it's more of an option. I was one of the younger cousins from my mother's side. They didn't really ask but now I feel like they ask cousins earlier. They ask earlier. They're more aware. I'm asking my cousins, "What are you going to do? What route are you going to do? What are you going to do? The junior college? Let me tell you what classes to take."

Now I'm on top of all of them, because I don't want them to feel scared, unmotivated. I want them to feel like they have support. I know what it was like for me. I know exactly what it was like.

The thing that defiantly helps the most is transferring over with support. With the Transfer Center, I was helping other students apply so I knew what it was going to be like for me to apply as well. I remember sitting down, when I was like, "Okay, here I go!" I knew it had to be local, if I wanted to keep the job that I had. It had to be local if I wanted to help my parents out with our restaurant still. I couldn't leave my parents behind. I felt like, "They wouldn't understand that." Nobody really ever did that. I don't regret it.

> *I knew it had to be local, if I wanted to keep the job that I had. It had to be local if I wanted to help my parents out with our restaurant still. I couldn't leave my parents behind.*

One time I did think about studying abroad for a semester in Italy. My mother cried just about the thought. Just thinking about what if something happened to me while I was over there. I was like, "Mom, I'll be fine. I'm not going by myself." And she cried about the thought and then again I had to hear the lecture, but one day I'll go.

I applied to Cal State Fullerton and to others just to see if I could be a candidate for them. I was able to get the application fee waiver so I could apply to four schools free of charge. I applied to Cal Poly Pomona, Cal State Fullerton; I also did San Diego, San Francisco. They were all California schools. I didn't consider anything out of state.

I didn't want to apply to any UC schools because when I took the classes, I just chose the Cal State system. I didn't consider UCs. I felt like I was gonna get the same education and of course my goal was Cal State Fullerton anyway so, I felt like I was going to get the same education but just for a different name. Not that there's anything wrong with the UC systems. They're just as great but I knew that the school of choice for me was going to be Cal States. They were going to be it, hopefully. UC Irvine is also pretty close in terms of distance but I don't feel like the UCs are for me. And none of my friends went to a UC, now that I think about it. Cal State Fullerton was my number one. And so, yeah with the case of IGETC, which one should I chose. I went the Cal State path.

When it came to me graduating from community college, I felt I had to walk in commencement. I had to do the ceremony otherwise my parents wouldn't believe that I graduated from here.

When it came to me graduating from community college, I felt I had to walk in commencement. I had to do the ceremony otherwise my parents wouldn't believe that I graduated from here. They didn't understand that it was a choice that you have to make. They thought you just eventually get your certificate. My friends, two of them didn't walk. I felt like I had to show my parents. This is the next step. I followed through. This is what I'm going to do next. I had to tell them what I had to do. I invited everybody to my graduation and everybody, luckily was able to come and see, "Okay, she really is done." If I would have told them, "Oh, I'm done." They'll be like, "No, you're not. You didn't graduate." Because they weren't really aware of it. I felt I had to show them this. Then they went, "Okay, so what's next?" Now I have to finish my classes for my Bachelor's Degree. I was like, "I finished everything else, the English, math, history, sciences. I finished all of that. I got my Associate's. I can probably get a better job maybe but I have to finish up over there. It's only two years. I am halfway. I had to explain to them because again, nobody went to the JC's.

My aunts were more understanding than my mom. It's funny because, maybe because they had better jobs, they knew that an education really was required. My mom used to work at a factory and used to work at a restaurant, so she wasn't really sur-

rounded by highly educated people. My aunts, they worked for
the city. They work for the City Manager. They work for a lot of
prestigious people at the city. They knew that an Associate's Degree really wasn't going to get me anywhere. Yes, a better job
but nothing as far as where they would like to see me one day.
They were like, "Okay, so what's next?" I said, "I'm going to finish up. I'm going to start my Bachelor's. It's only going to be two
years. After that, we'll see."

I knew I wanted to do Counseling. I thought I wanted to do
Counseling at the community college because of the Transfer
Center and the Career and Life Planning Center but then I realized, "Oh, what about therapy?" The longer that I was in school
I realized, "I want to do this with this population." With my
Bachelor's Degree, they required three internships, so I worked
with drug and alcohol abusers, with kids who have develop-
mental delays, and the third one was with at-risk youth. I
worked with kids, teens, and adults to see what I wanted to do.

I would tell them, "I'm going to graduate now. I'm going to
have internships so I'm going to see what I want to do. I'm not
sure yet." I didn't say, "This is the title I eventually want to have
one day" 'cuz I wasn't sure of that yet.

*I was really happy with my choice but again I had support
throughout the whole way. If it had been any different,
I would probably still be at community college.*

I was really happy with my choice but again I had support
throughout the whole way. If it had been any different, I would
probably still be at community college. I was close with my
friends. We did it together. Otherwise, it would have taken me
longer. What if they would have all gotten full-time jobs? Then
I would have probably applied full-time at the city. Unfortunately, that's probably where I would have been but luckily
that's not me. It works for other people. I think that's great. As

long as you finish within a reasonable timeline but being motivated is hard by yourself. Afterward you feel burned out.

I never allowed myself to take a semester off, otherwise that would have killed my motivation too. I've seen that happen a lot. My friends say, "Okay, I'm going to take one semester off." You just don't apply again. You get comfortable with the money. You get comfortable with the full-time work and the benefits and the health insurance. I had to be a full-time student to have health insurance with my mom's factory. Then my mom's company moved and she only stayed with the restaurant that we have. Then I didn't have health benefits. I still don't have health benefits.

Unfortunately, if you're part-time, they don't give you benefits. If I get a toothache, I have to go to Mexico for a cavity filling, but everything is not going to be a pretty picture now. It's an empty canvas. You have to paint as you go. In reality nobody guarantees you anything. Just because one person did it, the same thing isn't going to apply to you. Everybody has different circumstances.

Another thing that my friends and I would do is look up teachers. If they were good teachers I would take that class, even if it interfered with my schedule. To this day, if I have to come in the middle of the day, just for one class, I'll do it because if the teacher's not motivated, I'm not motivated. If the teacher doesn't care about the students, doesn't care if you show up, is filing through papers to see where they left off on the syllabus, doesn't remember what they talked about last week, that makes me think she doesn't care, so I don't care or if he doesn't care, I don't care. Unfortunately, it's that motivation again, that support again. If the teacher's like, "We follow the syllabus. There's a test next week." You feel prepared. I don't like a surprise pop quiz. I want to feel like I'm prepared for those. I still look up instructors to this day. I look up the teachers. If it's a bad teacher, I'll take it next semester.

*To this day, if I have to come in the middle of the day, just for
one class, I'll do it because if the teacher's not motivated,
I'm not motivated. If the teacher doesn't care about the
students, doesn't care if you show up, is filing through papers
to see where they left off on the syllabus, doesn't remember
what they talked about last week, that makes me think she
doesn't care, so I don't care or if he doesn't care, I don't care.*

I was admitted to all four universities that I applied to, luckily. I knew from my experience with my mom when I told her that I was thinking about going to Italy that first semester, that if I told her that I wanted to go to San Diego State and live on campus, then it would have scared her too much. She said one time, "What if one day you get sick in the middle of the night, who's going to be there to help you." She felt like I was divorcing her for some reason. Nobody had done that. I didn't want to do that to her. I did not want my mom to feel like I was going to go party in San Diego. That's not really my thing. I knew I didn't want to do that. My now-uncle did Human Services. He told me so much about the program. I read about it. And also, the advisor from the Human Services Department came to one of my classes at the community college and talked about the program. I felt like that's the way I wanted to go. That's what I wanted to do.

I already knew I would go to Cal State Fullerton. Yeah, especially because I looked it up. I asked questions. I didn't know so much about San Diego or San Francisco or Cal Poly, I didn't really ask. I felt like once I got there, I'll just get there. My heart was already set on Fullerton. That's what I wanted to do. I was okay with it. I wasn't going to be all sad because I didn't go to San Francisco or whatever. I was so close to my family. I would have been homesick. I would have eventually wanted to move back anyways. And I wasn't going to take my friends with me, for whatever reason they chose Fullerton too. I felt like I came in with them, I'm going to leave with them. It's been working for me alright. I made it through all of these challenges with them so it's working for me. This is what I'm going to do.

When it was time to leave the community college, as a student it made me feel like, "Wow! I graduated again. Wow! I've got something to show for myself." I felt like I was now really prepared to face the university. To me university was such a big word. I felt like, "Okay, I graduated. I did this, so I can do the other." I saw that I was able to accomplish it so I can accomplish other things as well. I felt happy but I felt like. "This is it. This is the real world."

I wasn't sure where I wanted to work or who I wanted to do things with but I knew that I loved how community college worked out for me so I wanted to be a counselor at the community college. I felt like this is it, the real world. You're really going to have more bills now. You're really going to have bigger bosses, more educated people around you, but I was excited for that. I was excited to see how I would dress up for work because of that one day I thought about it. "How do you envision yourself at work one day?" That one powerful statement really stuck with me because we even talked about it like twice. And mind you, this was on our way to working at the restaurant. It was on the freeway and that question, "So how do you envision yourself?" I was like, "I don't know."

As a kid I thought I was going to be a nurse. But then I was like "No, too much blood and seeing people suffering. I don't know but I wanted to help people. I wanted to make a difference for them." And then I was like, "No, heels. No, a suit." That's what I wanted to do, so I felt like, okay, I graduated high school. A lot of my friends didn't graduate high school, a high school that really didn't require much. I graduated high school. I graduated community college. I can graduate. I knew that I was going to be able to do it.

Luckily or not, my first semester was the hardest for me.
I got 3 'A's and a 'B', the rest, pure 'A's, the whole way!

A friend once told me, "If you get 'C's at the community college, you're probably going to get 'D's at the university." He told
me, it was going to be one grade level lower. He's like, "If you
get 'A's here, you get 'B's over there." Luckily or not, my first
semester was the hardest for me. I got 3 'A's and a 'B', the rest,
pure 'A's, the whole way! I was like "No, I'm going to do this."
I felt like, "Oh, it's going to be tough!" I was like "I don't care. I
can do it. I can do it." I have self-motivation now.

I know what I want to do. This is what I want to do. Once I
finished community college, I could finish the university. Then
when I graduated there, I was like "Okay, the real world again."
Cuz I never got another job. I stayed with the city. I'm still with
the city but I'm able to move up in the city now that I have my
Bachelor's Degree. Again I'm staying part-time because full-time
is school. That is my number one. If for whatever reason I get
laid off from the city, I can go back and work at my dad's restaurant, help him with that and still go to school.

Nothing is going to stop me now. I needed to graduate twice.
Now I graduated the third time. My Master's is next. I got this!

I'm 23 and they don't understand that. I don't want
them to feel like I'm disrespecting them but I want them
to understand me. I try to talk to them. They don't
understand that. I'm going to do this for my parents.

To celebrate my Bachelor's, I threw a big party. There were
150 people at a hall. With a band and everything! I was so happy!
I wasn't sure if I was going to get my Master's yet when I was
planning the party. I was like, "Well, maybe, I'm not going to go
to school for a while so let's make it big!" While we were making
arrangements for the party, I found out that I got accepted to the

Master's program. I was like "Oh my gosh, an even bigger reason to celebrate!" So yeah, my family has always been very supportive. I've never gotten a negative comment but as far as negativity, I think the only thing I received was, "It's going to be harder, and it's going to be harder".

Luckily nobody ever told me, "You're thinking too high" or "You're a woman, you can't do it" because it was expected for me to go to school.

There was a moment of rebellion when I was in high school. There was a disconnection from my parents. Because I was involved in school, they thought I was not supporting the family as much as I could. I felt like I was going to prove you wrong, that I wasn't really that rebellious a child. I did go to school. I was the one that had the higher grades because of Cheer. If you wanted to be a cheerleader, you had to pass all your classes. You had to make sure you didn't ditch. That helped me. I was always the one with the higher grades out of all my siblings. I was always the one that was more involved in school. But my father felt like I was betraying him. He didn't understand that. So I stopped working at the restaurant with him my senior year of high school and got a job at Chuck E. Cheese's.

My dad felt like it was a slap in the face because I had dances, football events and all these events on Saturdays. I couldn't help him. When I got a job, he felt like I betrayed him. So I was like, you know what? I'm going to let him see that what I'm doing is really for myself and for him because I feel like one day I will have to take care of my mother. Honestly, out of all of my siblings, I think I'm the one who is going to take care of my parents. I was like, you know what? I know what I'm doing is not really wrong.

I'm 23 and they don't understand that. I don't want them to feel like I'm disrespecting them but I want them to understand me. I try to talk to them. They don't understand that. I'm going to do this for my parents.

When I graduated, they were so proud and so happy. My dad got over the fact; he used to get so upset at me. Then I got the job at the city. He was so happy. All of a sudden he says his daughter works for the city. Then I graduated and all of a sudden he told all his friends, "Oh yeah, my daughter graduated." Then now I'm going to finish my Master's. He's like, "Yeah, my daughter this and that."

I'm the one who he thought rebelled the most. I have better jobs than both my brother and sister. Now I'm going to be more educated then all of my cousins from my mother's side of the family.

I did have to do things that he didn't understand. That both my parents didn't understand but I felt like they were there for me. I wasn't going to stop myself from doing these things. Unfortunately, I wasn't able to do the Italy trip, but I know that one day I'm going to go and be like, "Mom I went. Or let's go." Now I have a lot of self-motivation.

Now my dad doesn't have to tell me to wake up and go to school. Now I have their name engraved on my class ring. He's more proud of me, you could tell. Whenever my brother can't pay his bills he's like, "Why don't learn like your sister? She knows."

There was a time when my dad hardly even spoke to me.
Of course I'm not going to tell him that now,
cuz that really was a down time in my life
but I was trying to find my identity.

There was a time when my dad hardly even spoke to me. Of course I'm not going to tell him that now, cuz that really was a down time in my life but I was trying to find my identity. I didn't want to lose my girlfriends. I really wanted to live my life to the fullest my last year of high school. They didn't understand that. They didn't have that. My father, both my parents only had an elementary education. Now they know what it is all about. They're not worried about me now. I have a younger brother. He's going to be a sophomore this year in high school, so they're more focused on that right now. They know I'm fine. I don't want to remind them that there was a time when they didn't speak to me.

I'd like to help Latina families understand these issues and what kids are going through. It is something completely different. To help parents understand. To work on communication issues. That's what I felt that I lacked with my parents because it was just what my father said. Its like, "Why don't you try to meet me halfway?" So, that's where I am. I want to help Hispanic families if I can.

That is the reason I wanted to work with at-risk youth because there really is a cultural-age issue. Parents say, "When I was young, we didn't do that kind of stuff" but unfortunately, we're not where you were. We're not. Things change. Cuz you don't hear people, Hispanic people, really seeking therapy. I'd like to help Latina families understand these issues. What kids are going through. It is something completely different. To help parents understand. To work on communication issues. That's what I felt that I lacked with my parents because it was just what my father said. Its like, "Why don't you try to meet me halfway?" So, that's where I am. I want to help Hispanic families if I can.

Usually they go to a cousin's house and its like, "Can you talk to my son?" In reality maybe you do need professional help. Or the father's an alcoholic. They think that one day he'll leave it or he's a social drinker. No, there really are problems behind that. That's where I stand.

That was a low time in my life that helped me. I'm going to prove you wrong. Unfortunately, it had to be towards my parents but til this day, I help them out. I don't want them to think negative about me. When in reality, I'm doing a little better than everybody else. I don't want to point fingers like, "Look at me, look at them, look how you treated my brother, look how you treated my sister."

I am their first daughter to go to college. My sister at this age already had 3 kids. I don't even have one. I'm not even married or close to being married. I learned in school that educated women don't have a lot of kids. Don't have 10 kids, 10-15 kids. You can't do that here now. It's too expensive but I would love to one day have my family. I tell my mom, I'm not ready for that yet. I want to be financially secure. I want to be educated so I can educate my kids right. Of course, take some of the values that they showed me but not everything. I am not going to make my kids work at age 12. I'm sure they did it with no harm intended. No harm intended and it helped me out.

I don't like to live with regrets to think, this is what you did to me. You scared me. I've been working since the age of 12 but I think that's helped me. I see those points in my life as something good. I learned from them. I'm going to keep going from there. As far as for school, I needed support from my girlfriends. Cuz my parents didn't know. That's all mine.

To be successful in school, you need motivation. You need to ask questions. You need to do your own research as far as looking up your teachers, what classes you have to take.

We need support and family asking, "How are you doing in school?" They don't need to be telling you what to do. Simply asking and them saying, "Good job, keep it up!" That's all you need to hear.

We need support and family asking, "How are you doing in school?" They don't need to be telling you what to do. Simply asking and them saying, "Good job, keep it up!" That's all you need to hear.

I speak for myself but your parents ask for a lot. They ask for a lot. You're expected to help them out once you graduate from high school. Parents need to understand you. They don't know what it is like because maybe they didn't go to college. You have to surround yourself with people that will help you, as far as your school, the Counseling Center.

With the family, you're still expected to follow the family rules. It's that untold rule, an unsaid rule, "You have to obey what your parents say" and help them out in any way because they're getting older and weak. Parents need to understand a little bit more that there's times that you have to stay up til midnight, studying for midterms because there's going to be 3 or 4 this week. And my dad would send me to bed, "Go to sleep." So I had to wake up at 5 in the morning the next day to study.

I see community college as such a positive experience for me. I really enjoyed it here. Looking back, I would have been more involved in clubs. I didn't join any clubs. I would have been more involved in clubs or would have attended more school events but because I was working here and coming to class here, I was done with the campus after being on campus for 11 hours. I just wanted to go home. I did a good job of looking up the teachers. I love the fact that I worked at the Transfer Center and the Career and Life Planning Center. They can be on my resume. That looks so good! Before, Chuck E. Cheese's was the only job I had.

I did a good job about getting jobs on campus and getting good professors. I didn't really see it as something negative. Then I met my boyfriend here. He tells me to this day, "If it wasn't for you, I never would have transferred." He would have dropped out. A dropout like all his other friends.

You don't waste your time in community college but you need to make sure you take the right classes with good teachers. I really enjoyed my work experience here. It really helped me transfer over. And transferring over in a group is a great thing, not doing it by yourself.

Many times, Latina families expect so much more from a man then they do from a woman in the household. They feel that the man can be the only bread winner. The woman can only be the stay at home mom. It's just acculturation issues. It is a very big topic. A topic that should always be talked about. Students need to talk about home life, "How's it at home for you?" That question alone can boil up so much due to acculturation issues. There's nothing really wrong with it but you have to be able to work with it.

Latina women are people who do so much. They have to juggle so many balls yet they do it and put on a show while they're at it. I'm happy to be Latina! I'm so happy! I don't want to change my last name. It's so Mexican! We're so capable!

Latina women are people who do so much. They have to juggle so many balls yet they do it and put on a show while they're at it. I'm happy to be Latina! I'm so happy! I don't want to change my last name. It's so Mexican! We're so capable! A lot of people out there in the Hispanic community are worried because the women are coming up. The women are being educated. The man isn't the only bread winner anymore. Sometimes you do need to have both people working in order to carry the kids and pay the babysitter. My gosh, it's expensive!

We need to be proud. Be proud. I want my parents to be like, "Wow, there was a time where I honestly thought she was such a brat." One day they'll thank me. One day they'll thank me and I have them to thank. I mean, they paid for community college! I paid for Cal State but they paid for community college. They gave me a job that I had since I was 12. Because of my parents, I learned to have priorities. I know how to work out my days. I really thank them for everything. I don't regret anything. Anytime something bad happened in my life, it made me stronger.

It didn't kill me, it made me stronger. We're capable of doing a lot of things. Not only Latina women, women in general.

Profile Update: Anais transferred to the California State University, Fullerton and graduated with her Bachelor's Degree. She was last known to be in the process of completing her Master's Degree at the California State University, Fullerton.

Chapter Seven
Dad's Right Hand

I've never been able to see my future self anywhere. That's why I always felt that I was weird. I have always known that I would get to where I wanted to go, regardless of whether or not I picture it in my head. You know how little girls picture their wedding? I don't do that. I set a goal and I get there. I was a very good student in high school. I graduated with a 3.51 GPA. I took AP courses. I took the literature AP exam for Spanish. That alone helped me a lot.

In getting to community college, I took a year and a half off from high school, then I came to college. When I got to community college, I already knew what I wanted to do. I wanted to get my classes. Get it done. Then graduate and move on. It took me five years to do that.

*When I got to community college, I already knew what
I wanted to do. I wanted to get my classes. Get it done.
Then graduate and move on. It took me five years to do that.*

The first semester I took only one class. I knew that if I took four classes, I would set myself up to fail. I didn't want to do that. I wanted to take a class. Take it a day at a time. A semester at a time. Which I did. I did fine my first semester here. Then the next consecutive three semesters after that, I would take four classes but I would drop three. I would keep one class. That was a bad pattern, so I got put on academic probation. That made me realize that I couldn't fool around, because I needed to go to school. And I love school!

As far as family, my dad was very supportive. My dad has always pushed us to be our best and pursue higher education. Within my family, on my mom's side, they're all doctors, politicians, and education is not a question for them. I grew up with my aunt for three years, she emphasized education a lot. That was a building block for me and my sister.

When we came here with our parents to the U.S. from Mexico, my dad was very pushy about school. Doing well. Being very supportive about high school and activities. Attending the meetings. That alone made me realize that my dad was not only pushing us, but really wanted to be there for us. That helped. Later when my sister graduated from high school, we both started college at the same time. That was a blessing. We both encouraged one another to take classes and really motivate one another that way. My dad was very supportive about it all.

When I first came to community college, I was ready to come here. I was ready to go to school, as opposed to just being a senior who recently graduated from high school. I don't think I was ready at that time, to be honest. When I got here after taking time off, I was motivated. I wanted to succeed. I wanted to do well. It was a positive experience for me. I can't say anything negative about that.

When I was placed on academic probation, I felt very, very bad. I thought I was letting my dad down. I was letting my family down. 'Cuz we're very connected; we're very close. If I fail, then I feel like they're going to feel like they're failing as well. Especially my dad 'cuz he's a single parent. That was very hard for me. That was my motivation almost. It made me feel really horrible about what I was doing, taking classes and dropping them. Also the money, I mean, that was money going to the trash can. I felt really bad about that. That alone motivated me to get out of it. After that, if you've seen my transcript- it's A's and B's, mostly A's. I've been doing really well.

When I was placed on academic probation, I felt very,
very bad. I thought I was letting my dad down.
I was letting my family down. 'Cuz we're very connected;
we're very close. If I fail, then I feel like they're
going to feel like they're failing as well.

When I told my dad I was put on academic probation, he wasn't mad. He was very understanding. He asked me why. I gave him my reasons. Then he said, "Maybe you wanna try harder. I can help you. I can get in contact with people. I can come with you to one of the centers they have there." He was very willing to come with me so I could succeed. I said that I would do it on my own. I knew what I needed to do. I didn't need my dad to hold my hand. I did it on my own. Then I came to the Transfer Center two semesters after that. I got the help that I needed there. I got the support system that I needed as far as information about transferring, talking to the UC representatives, and going through my transcript, really understanding what the units mean, and the system itself. How to get out of the system. And really work the system. That's what I learned being there at the Transfer Center.

Coming to community college my first semester, I knew I wanted to study psychology and go to medical school. That was my ultimate goal. There was no way that I would change my mind, throughout the years. That really gave me a foundation to continue working on that. On that ultimate goal. Which I did. I took Psychology 101 with Julie Folander. Her class absolutely motivated me. It literally changed my life. I knew that's what I wanted to do. To see the fire in her, in her eyes, the way she would teach the class. That really captivated me and motivated me to do what she was doing. I knew I didn't want to be a teacher. I want to be a therapist or to study the brain. I know I want to go to medical school. That was easy, it came very easy. It really wasn't very challenging at all.

I took Psychology 101 with Julie Folander. Her class absolutely motivated me. It literally changed my life. I knew that's what I wanted to do. To see the fire in her, in her eyes, the way she would teach the class. That really captivated me and motivated me to do what she was doing. I knew I didn't want to be a teacher. I want to be a therapist or to study the brain.

When it came to looking at colleges to transfer to, I had a cousin who went to UC Irvine. Not a blood cousin but he's been in the family. He would always talk about UCI, that's where he wanted to go. I would drive by UCI when I was little, so I always thought in the back of my head, "Well, UCI sounds like a reasonable idea."

Then I started looking at other options, because here at the Transfer Center, I was advised not to look at just one school. So that's what I did. I looked at the Cal States, both Cal State Fullerton and Cal State Long Beach. I looked at their programs, as well as Chapman University. All those schools that I looked into, their programs were very strong in the psychology field. I gravitated to those ideas. Primarily I looked at UCI and Chapman University.

Chapman University because their classes are very small. They're like 30, 35 students at the most. In the back of my mind, I was thinking, "Well, I already did the community college experience. I did experience the big, large halls. I knew that if I didn't put myself out there, the teacher wasn't going to notice me." I did that. I put myself out there. That helped me to build a foundation with my teacher and communication with them. And a close bond. I was thinking if I go to Chapman, I won't just be another number. I'll be a person who stands out alone. I gravitated to that a lot. I looked into their psychology requirements in their program. I had the option to get a B.A. or a B.S. in psychology. The B.S. really grabbed my attention, given the fact that I want to go to medical school. I thought it was a great idea. Another reason why I wanna go there is because it's closer to home. I didn't want to move away to a different state or whatnot 'cuz I want to be closer to my family 'cuz I'm my dad's right hand. That helped as well.

Then I would take the university tours. I went on my own to the both campuses, UCI and Chapman University. I didn't really quite like the idea of the Cal States, because I never envisioned myself at a Cal State. Not to look down on them or anything, but I really wanted to go to a university. That was my ultimate dream. I knew I belonged there.

By visiting the campuses, I knew I would have no problem, even when I saw people that didn't really look like me, being Latina. That didn't really intimidate me. If anything, I saw that as an opportunity to learn about other people. To see if I could succeed in life. Because in life you're not just gonna be with a pool of people. You're gonna be with a whole bunch of other people, especially being here in California. I took it as a learning experience. It didn't intimidate me.

Because in life you're not just gonna be with a pool of people. You're gonna be with a whole bunch of other people, especially being here in California. I took it as a learning experience. It didn't intimidate me.

I visited Cal State Long Beach and Cal State Fullerton. I visited UC Irvine, Chapman University. The ones in San Diego, San Diego State and UC San Diego. I've been to Washington University. I love the campus up there but I didn't see myself moving away from my family. Especially the weather. Those were all the campuses that I visited.

When it came time to apply, I was living with my dad. My

dad told me, "Go for it. I will support you. If we need to move away, we will." He's always been very supportive like that.

I'm my dad's right hand. I'm 25 but I don't want to leave my dad yet because I don't want him to be alone. That's my main concern. I told my dad, "This is what I'm looking at." I laid it all out on the table. I said, "These are the colleges that I'm looking at. These are within the area. They're not very far. What do you think about it?" and he said, "Just do it. I will support you." I mean, he has so far. I didn't see my college choice as an obstacle for him. He said, "Just do whatever you can or what you wanna do. Just do it. I will support you no matter what." He's been like that with my brother, with my other sister. That's a blessing.

I've always believed that you become like the five people that you surround yourself with. By taking psychology, being interested in that field, I knew that I had to be very careful about my friends. My inner circle. I've been fortunate enough to have friends that wanna go places, that wanna achieve higher education, that are on the same path that I'm on, the same journey. That wasn't very hard. That was very easy. We would always talk about applying to the UC's, and what is your experience like or can you read my personal statement? Can you help me out? It's been very positive.

In terms of where I applied, I applied to UC Irvine, Chapman University, Cal State Fullerton, and Cal State Long Beach. I only applied to the Cal States because it was my plan B or C. I got accepted to all of them. But for UC Irvine, I missed the deadline for the Statement of Intent to Register. I was still waiting on Chapman University. Chapman University responded to me halfway through the month of June. The SIR for UC Irvine was due June 1st. I didn't do that thinking that I would absolutely get accepted to Chapman. That was the school that I would go to. Little did I know, I didn't really inform myself about tuition there. It's $32,000.

I got accepted to all of them. For UC Irvine, I missed the deadline for the Statement of Intent to Register. I was still waiting on Chapman University. Chapman University responded to me halfway through the month of June. The SIR for UC Irvine was due June 1st. I didn't do that thinking that I would absolutely get accepted to Chapman. That was the school that I would go to.

When I got my acceptance letter, they gave me a merit award of $12,000. $6,000 per semester. That was great! I was very happy to see that in the mail and to know that I got accepted. When I looked at the catalog that they sent me with my acceptance letter, it was $32,000. I didn't feel that I would get the money to go in the fall. When I told my dad, he said, "That's great that you got accepted. That's $12,000. Good for you! You're a great student!" I told him, "Unfortunately, I won't be able to go because we don't have enough money to go there." The same day that I let him know, I went to UC Irvine to file a late appeal.

Within a week I found out that I got denied on my appeal. That was very devastating to be honest. I didn't let that experience bring me down, which was for me to stay at home and not go to school. That was never an option for me. So what I did, I enrolled myself back in community college. Now I am taking another class here because I don't have any other requirements to meet. I'm taking one class. In the spring I'll be taking two classes. I will be applying again to the UC's and the Cal States in the fall.

After completing the transfer university applications the first time, it was positive but it was hectic at the same time. There are so many deadlines that you have to keep up with. So many little details that if you don't have a strong support system around you and people that are going through the same experience as you, you would probably feel lost in the system.

What I did was I came to the Transfer Center. I talked to John.

I talked to Vince. I talked to the people I was surrounded with, my friends. We were all going through a similar situation. That's where I got my support system, my foundation. They were the ones, especially John and Vince, who guided me through the process because I was completely lost. I didn't know how to do it. Also my sister, she was going through the same process as I was at the same time. We built that support system. That really gets people through the transfer experience.

My perspective of myself changed because I took a year-and-a-half off. I've always known that I wanted to go to a university and medical school, but I was never able to picture it in my head. When I started here, I was very green. Then the transfer experience happened. The five years that I spent here, that really built my character in the sense that going through the transfer experience helped me grow. I've been able to build my character a little stronger. I'm a go-getter. I don't have the luxury of sitting here, waiting for things to happen for me and for other people to do it for me. That's not college. College is when you gotta do it all on your own. A support system is great but you ultimately have to do it on your own.

I don't have the luxury of sitting here, waiting for things to happen for me and for other people to do it for me. That's not college. College is when you gotta do it all on your own. A support system is great but you ultimately have to do it on your own.

I feel that I can do anything, especially because I had to raise my little sister since she was the age of 1. She was 1 and 3 months when she came into our family. Being the oldest, I had to be the mom. My dad had to be the dad. Again, I'm my dad's right hand. I've always had that role in my family. That has shaped me, my character into being strong and being a go-getter.

I know I can do anything because of what I've gone through.

Because of being the mom of the family, because of raising the little girl, coming to school, doing homework, studying for exams, and doing well in school with a child. I know I can do anything. It might be very naïve of me to say, but I know I can do anything.

To be a success, I believe that you need to be persistent. You need to be very focused and very determined in what you gotta do, in what you want to do in the end. Have a goal in mind. Set higher goals and little goals at the same time. Because if you don't set yourself goals, then you're gonna go through your college experience and you're not gonna finish anything. For me, I set myself a goal.

Have a goal, then surround yourself with positive people. People that can get you there. People that know people that will get you there, that will help you, for example, the Transfer Center. Being here, the only people that come here are people who want to transfer. Knowing that, I know that I am in the right place. I started talking to people around the Transfer Center as my friends. If you surround yourself with positive people, people that have the same goal in mind, transferring and going to a UC, then you will become like them. You will adopt their behavior. You will adopt their ideals. Not to say that you don't have your own ideals, but you will become like the people you surround yourself with. I believe that if you surround yourself with positive people, you educate yourself, you do the research. If you have a question, ask questions. Any questions that you have, just ask questions, even if they sound silly. They're not silly 'cuz you don't know the answers. Don't be shy about being AB 540 or whatever obstacle that you think you have in your life. Overcome that obstacle because if you don't, you're just gonna sit here and waste your time.

Next time I apply to transfer, I am going to stay on top of the deadlines, and know when the next deadline is. And apply for scholarships, scholarships, scholarships! Being AB 540, I don't have the luxury to sit here and wait for the government to help me. I can't do that. I have to go out there, make the money, and finance my own education. I've been fortunate enough that my dad is there to help me.

Being AB 540, I don't have the luxury to sit here and wait for the government to help me. I can't do that. I have to go out there, make the money, and finance my own education.

Next time around, I'm gonna write my personal statement two months in advance, no waiting until November to write it. Also ask people to proofread it. I am not going to procrastinate because college students, we do that a lot. We leave things till the last minute, even though we know we need to do it sooner rather than later. We leave it till the last minute. Stay on top of things. Do not get frustrated. Because if I get overwhelmed, then I will lose my momentum, my focus.

To deal with that, I exercise. Outside of that, my family helps me. If I feel like I don't wanna get up to go to class, or I don't wanna get up to do it all over again, I'll think about my dad and my little sister. Those are my motivation, my drive. I see that I'm an example to my little sister. If I let myself go down, she will go down with me. So will my entire family. I don't wanna let my dad down. He wakes up at 5:00 in the morning to go to work; I can't wake up at 7:00 to go to school? I need to do what I have to do to be a good student. Those two, my sister and my dad, are definitely my motivation.

For sure, education begins at home. Not only at this level, at the college level, being a Latina and being an undocumented immigrant and being the oldest of the family, we need to educate our people younger, like in high school. Letting our parents know what's going on. We need that. Maybe here at the Transfer Center, they can have like a Parent Night or something that the parents are exposed to what their kids are going through.

Oftentimes they feel very detached. Because they feel like, "Oh, they're going to school. That has nothing to do with me." I hear it from other students and my friends here at school. They would share their stories, "My mom thinks I'm going to school because I don't wanna be at home or go to work or for whatever reason." Parents don't feel really connected with the children because they feel they're at a different level. The children don't know how to connect with their parents at home. By educating the parents, maybe more Latinos will go to college. More Latinos will achieve higher education. Just having that support system at home really helps. I mean that's been my experience.

I hear it from other students and my friends here at school. They would share their stories, "My mom thinks I'm going to school because I don't wanna be at home or go to work or for whatever reason." Parents don't feel really connected with the children because they feel they're at a different level. The children don't know how to connect with their parents at home.

It really depends on the dynamics of the family. I've only known my family and my experience. It's been very positive. I feel blessed like that. But for other families and for other kids or other young adults that don't have their parents with them or live in a single parent home or who don't have a support system, educating parents is important. It is still possible now, even at this level. Even if you're 20 years old. Even if you're 25 or 27 and you're still here. If you expose your parents to that, the parents would understand a little better. They will empathize with that.

For me, my family is my motivation. If you have a support system here as well as at home, that will really drive people to do well in the future and succeed in attaining higher education. If you have that support here, you will have that association with you to get that support later in life. It will be easier for you as a student.

Being an undocumented immigrant, with the whole AB 540 thing, not many people off-campus two years ago knew what AB 540 was. Even the faculty. You would bring it up to their attention and the teachers, they wouldn't know what you were talking about. Awareness, education, having the information really helps tremendously. It changes everything if your teachers know what is going on. You will have your positives and negatives about exposing your immigration status to people. Educating people in general helps in anything or in any subject if you want to educate the public. With the teachers, if you educate them, then they will understand their students. They will be a little more sympathetic about it. They will help the students more. For example, for me, being AB 540, I would let my professors know, "Hey I'm not getting help from the government, but I still wanna take your class. I don't have enough money for the books but maybe we can work something out." And, they do. They loan you the books. Teachers want you to succeed. I mean, if you don't let them know your situation or you don't speak up, then you're not gonna be heard. That's with everything.

For me, being AB 540, I would let my professors know, "Hey I'm not getting help from the government, but I still wanna take your class. I don't have enough money for the books but maybe we can work something out." And, they do. They loan you the books. Teachers want you to succeed. I mean, if you don't let them know your situation or you don't speak up, then you're not gonna be heard. That's with everything.

Over the past three semesters, I've seen a big change in regards to the AB 540 awareness on campus. Now people are a little more aware. With that, if we continue to educate our professors and the population here on campus about any other subject, or any other matter, they will be a little more open to it. They won't be oblivious to what is happening in their community.

Here at this community college, we have the best professors, the best staff and people want students to succeed. The teachers want you to succeed as a student. Because of my experience over the past 5 years, I've learned that if you don't reach out to them, they won't reach back to you. They are willing to help. Everybody on campus is here to help!

Latinas need to know that we can do it! The community college is not a broken system. It is a structured system. You can make it work in a way tailored to you, the individual. Educating yourself and doing the research, and surrounding yourself with positive people and really educating yourself about it, you will succeed. Community college is not bad. It saves you some money!

Profile update: Desi transferred to the California State University, Fullerton and graduated with her Bachelor of Science Degree in Psychology in 2016.

Chapter Eight
Get a High School Diploma and Don't Get Pregnant

I had been going on college fieldtrips since high school. I was a part of what was called the Puente Program in my high school. We were always being pushed towards the university, but it didn't sink in until my senior year in high school. We went on a trip to northern California. They usually did it during our junior year but because of budget cuts we had to wait 'til our senior year. We were staying at the UC Berkeley campus. I remember sitting there and thinking, "I could go here. You know, it's possible." But then, sometimes I'm a very negative person. I was like, "Yeah right, that's impossible." I shook it away from my mind. As graduation came nearer, I had no idea what I was going to do. Am I going to go to college or university? It was already May. People had already applied to schools. Deadlines had passed. I was stuck. "Okay, well," I thought, "I'm getting my high school diploma." That was my only goal during high school, get a high school diploma and don't get pregnant. All the women in my family were single mothers. They got pregnant when they were teenagers. It was not necessarily that I didn't have goals for myself, but I always thought I'd follow that pattern. Like it was destiny.

All the women in my family were single mothers. They got pregnant when they were teenagers. It was not necessarily that I didn't have goals for myself, but I always thought I'd follow that pattern. Like it was destiny.

For the longest time, I always thought to myself, "When I graduate from high school, I'm going to be working to support my kid."

I was in the Puente Program because when they promoted it I was like, "Oh, cool! Being in a classroom full of Latinos and being exposed to Latino authors." I love reading, so that was the main thing. Not because of college or the university. I got to go on cool fieldtrips and learn about Hispanic authors. When the end time came, I had friends that were like, "Oh my God! I got accepted here or I'm doing this!" I was like, "Oh my God, what am I going to do with my life? I have a choice. I have got to do something." It was during May when I decided about going to college.

Someone told me there's something called community college. "You can go to a community college. There's one in the next town over. It's not that far away, you can go there." I applied that morning. I went into one of the classrooms at my high school to do the online application for community college because I didn't have a computer at home. Even here at community college, for the longest time I didn't have a computer. They told me, "You can use the classroom computer. You don't have to sit in class today. You can go to my office and apply." That's when I really pictured myself in college, "Oh, my gosh, I'm going to college!" It was when I filled out the application to community college.

Before I got there, I imagined college as this amazing place. It sounded like a fairy tale. College! Yet when I got here, you realized it's manageable. It's not as chaotic as I imagined. "Oh my goodness, I'm going to this far away land! I'm going to get to learn about more authors. I'm going to get to write!" Books were always my thing. I ended up being an English major. I think it was destined.

Before I got there, I imagined college as this amazing place.
It sounded like a fairy tale. College! Yet when I got here,
I realized it's manageable. It's not as chaotic as I imagined.

In the high school Puente Program, I imagined myself in college for a brief moment but I didn't allow myself to think about it too much. For me, I thought, "No, get it out of your head. You're going to be disappointed and find out you're pregnant."

I'm the first college-bound person in my family. College was something you would hear about but it wasn't something for my family to consider. "You could either keep going to school or else get a job. We just gotta pay the rent." There was never a real push, like "You gotta go to college. You gotta get a degree." It was more like, "Get your high school diploma so you can get a job. We can pay the rent." I don't feel like my family pushed college and even universities. When it was time to transfer, they were like, "I have no idea what you're talking about. Don't talk to me about that."

When I applied to community college that morning, I went home. My mom was the only one at the house. I told her that I was going to community college. She was like, "Oh, that's cool." And that was pretty much it. When it came time to complete the FAFSA, there was an announcement that they were gonna have a workshop at my high school. That's when I had to be like, "Mom, you gotta get off of work early. You need to go with me to this place." That's when it started to become real, when I asked for the tax forms. I was asking for everything so I could find a computer and fill it out. She didn't fill out any of the forms with me. I filled out all of the financial stuff myself.

I remember feeling guilty during that period of time. I have so many strong, working women around me. What makes me think I deserve to go to college? Because it's a privilege. College is a privilege. I felt like I was bothering her to ask for anything.

I felt like I was making it seem like I'm better than them or something. As if I was trying to make myself feel superior because there is this place called college. I know more than you do.

I felt like my mom was hesitant about me going because she didn't know much about it. She was concerned. She felt guilty not being able to guide me. She would say, "Ask your teachers. See if you can get help from this professor or that professor."

Before I started at the community college, I went to the Financial Aid Office. I was terrified when I found out how much college cost. I was given guidance and found out about these grants that'll cover the cost. When I found out about financial aid, it was like, "Oh my God, I'm gonna get paid to learn!" It was an amazing concept to me.

> *When I found out about financial aid, it was like,*
> *"Oh my God, I'm gonna get paid to learn!"*
> *It was an amazing concept to me.*

The first day of classes, I found out that you had to register online. I didn't find that out at Orientation, in my Group Advising. I was told to register for classes, but I thought there was a counselor that does that for you. So the first day of school, I was nervous because I wasn't sure if I was going to get any classes. I called the Registration Office to ask them, "Hey, how do I know my schedule? How do I find this out?" It was past the deadline to add classes. The classes were all full. I had to petition to add classes late. I was so scared that I wasn't even going to get to attend college my first semester!

On the first day of the fall semester, the first class I tried to get into was an English class. The classroom I went to was full so I had to find another English class. There was this girl who had her class schedule. She said, "We can go to another class and try it out." I followed her. We ran to find another class. That's how I met my English professor, Heather Richards. I took all her classes ever since that day. I felt welcomed by her. Just her introduction made me feel so comfortable, like I was in the right place for me. I knew that was it. My first semester I had her class. She guided me the entire way through. She was my first class, my first college experience, my first mentor. Once classes started, I felt like I was supposed to be there.

We ran to find another class. That's how I met my English professor, Heather Richards. I took all her classes ever since that day. I felt welcomed by her. Just her introduction made me feel so comfortable, like I was in the right place for me. I knew that was it. My first semester I had her class. She guided me the entire way through. She was my first class, my first college experience, my first mentor.

One day after the end of the second year at community college, I saw everyone lined up with their caps and gowns. I was like, "Oh my God! I didn't apply to transfer anywhere! I should be graduating." But because I was undecided, I was taking my time. I was a full-time student but I hadn't figured out my major yet. The third year is when I really got active. I decided to transfer.

I was gonna go to Cal State Fullerton. I fulfilled my classes. I fulfilled those requirements. Cal State's down the street. I don't drive, so I'll be able to take the bus. Plus, I could manage it economically. Cal State Fullerton was it. It was Octoberish. End of November is the deadline.

I kept walking to the cafeteria during those months. I would see the signs out here in front of the Transfer Center. The signs advertised the university representative is gonna be here. We have this workshop or we'll help with personal statements. I thought "Personal statements? I don't think I need one for Cal State Fullerton." But I started really questioning myself, "Well, maybe I should find out more." Thankfully I had a lot of guidance from Janine. Janine, from the Career Center. She guided me the whole way too. Her and my co-worker, they were like, "You're gonna go to Cal State Fullerton? That's great!" My co-worker actually attended Cal State Fullerton. They even told me, "You have so much potential. Why don't you apply to a UC? Why don't you apply to all of them?" I was gonna go to Cal State. I knew it. I didn't apply because I went through so much depression.

When it was time to apply, there was a two-week span where Janine and my co-worker were just like, "Did you apply yet? Are you going to apply? Do you have your personal statement?" And I was like, "Oh, I'll do it tomorrow." I kept pushing it off because I was depressed. I was too scared to even apply or write a personal statement.

The prompt is something like, "Share something about yourself or your leadership." I was surprised at how hard it is to write about myself. I felt like, "Am I even worthy to go to a Cal State or a UC. What am I doing? I'm lucky to be going to a community college. I was supposed to get an Associate's. Get into the working world. Help pay the rent. I need to help the family. What do I think I'm doing? I already did three years here. That should be it. I don't need to go anywhere else." Janine had gone on vacation so I was alone in the Career Center. She kept calling and asking me, "Have you applied yet? Are you gonna apply?"

I finally broke down to my co-worker two days before it was time to apply. I was like, "I haven't even written a personal statement. I don't know what to do. I don't feel like I am good enough. What am I doing? What if everything I've done up to now isn't good enough?" She had seen my transcripts. I had decided English was going to be my major. I had straight A's. I had the grades and the right classes. Emotionally, I didn't have the belief in myself. I didn't feel like I deserved it. "Who am I to be going to the University of California?"

She had seen my transcripts. I decided English was going to be my major. I had straight A's. I had the grades and the right classes. Emotionally, I didn't have the belief in myself. I didn't feel like I deserved it.

I decided, "Well, let me look at the writing prompt again." My co-worker was like, "Just answer it freely. Just type. Just start typing. From there I'll help you." I typed it up. Work closes at 5:00pm. I said, "Tomorrow I'll show it to you." I left. Then I came over to the Transfer Center. There were a ton of students there. The staff was really overwhelmed. They said, "We're only going to see two more personal statements." It was already who knows what time at night, 9:00pm? I was like, "Okay, I'll just leave." I guess the Transfer Center had been having workshops all semester. I was like, "How embarrassing. How am I going to take this rough, rough draft to them? They've been seeing incredible applications and personal statements this whole time? I'm not even gonna waste my time." I went home.

That night I get home and Janine's calling my cell phone, "Did you apply yet? Where's your personal statement?" That night I really decided "This is it. I need to apply."

The following day, it was November 30th. The day where everything's due. I showed my personal statement to my co-worker. She has two jobs. She had to go to her other job. She had me email it to her. She edited everything for me and rewrote some sections. When I reread the personal statement that she sent me of myself, I started crying. I felt like, "Oh my God! Who is this person? She really thinks I'm that great? It was amazing!" I got the application fee waiver, thank God. Also, I applied to four Cal States. I applied to Long Beach, Cal State Fullerton, Dominguez Hills, I believe, and then some other random Cal State. For the UC's, I applied to Irvine, LA, Berkeley, and San

Diego. I applied to everything. I was just like, "Okay, well, whatever happens happens."

I was still majorly depressed even when I hit the submit button. "What if I don't get into anywhere? What am I going to do? How embarrassing!" Janine knows that I applied. What am I going to tell her when they tell me I wasn't accepted? They told me, "Let it go. They're gonna take you. Don't worry about it. You have the grades. You have the potential. Don't worry about it."

Thankfully when I was applying, I had been active in Latina Leadership Network here on campus so I felt good when it was like, "Have you done community service or have you been involved in anything?" Because I felt like I've been helping the community. Maybe they'll see that I've been doing my hours. They'll see I've been working. I work 20 hours each week, getting extensions on my work study award amounts. They've given me so many extensions. I've had so much help. Maybe they'll see that I really want this.

That was the application season. Major depression. Major, I have no idea where I'm going. Huge procrastination! They believed in me when I didn't believe in myself. They pushed me. If it wasn't for them, I probably wouldn't have applied to anywhere.

That was the application season. Major depression. Major,
I have no idea where I'm going. Huge procrastination.
They believed in me when I didn't believe in myself.
They pushed me. If it wasn't for them,
I probably wouldn't have applied to anywhere.

Really what helped me in the application process was a bunch of things, like people pushing me. Even the sign that the Transfer Center puts out there by the cafeteria. It is a daily reminder like, "Oh my gosh, it's application season." You know, those little reminders make you question, am I capable? It makes you think, "Am I capable? Can I do this? Am I worthy?" But it was nice.

Also, thankfully, I was a work-study student for a counselor so I was aware of the university admission requirements. Even though I felt like, maybe I wasn't going to transfer. I was told, you follow IGETC. You need to follow it. Even if you decide you're going to get an Associate's Degree only. You'll go to Cal State or whatever you have planned; you follow IGETC because you never know. I followed IGETC really closely. My counselor would periodically check on me. Poor guy. I broke down in his office so many times, like, "I don't know what I'm doing in college. I don't know what I'm going to do with my life. I don't know what to major in." There was so much confusion. Following IGETC was good.

In applying to different schools, the deciding factor was the name. Being around school people, being around different people. Hearing words like Berkeley or UCLA. USC was my dream school. The application deadline was in February. I did not have time to apply at all. I did not apply because of that depression. It got so heavy. One time I came in to the Transfer Center. I asked "Can I see what it takes to transfer to USC?" I believe it was Vince who helped me with it. He gave me a print out. Here are some of the questions they might ask you. I went to the library. They had questions like "Do you have any family that went to USC or do you know this or do you know that?" While I was reading the application I was like, "I don't know anyone. They're not gonna take me. I don't have money." I let the depression get to me. I didn't tell anyone that I wanted to apply there or that I always dreamed of USC. I didn't apply. That's my one regret.

While I was reading the application I was like, "I don't know
anyone. They're not gonna take me. I don't have money."
I let the depression get to me. I didn't tell anyone that I
wanted to apply there or that I always dreamed of USC.
I didn't apply. That's my one regret.

As for my family, at first, I told them I was thinking about
going to Cal State Fullerton. When I told them later that I applied
to all these universities, they were like, "Oh well, how far is that?
Why are you going to go there when you could take the courses
at Cal State Fullerton?"

My dad wasn't always in the picture. When I was at the
community college, all this family drama happened. I found
myself living with my mom and her husband, plus my dad, and
all of us in this one house. Family situations occurred. My
brother got caught up in gang-related activity and got locked
up. In order to lessen his time, my family had to show that we
were going to move away from the city. My mom was able,
thankfully, to find a house in the next town over. Economically
the house wasn't affordable, so we had to all move in together.
It was my mother's new boyfriend at the time, my mom, me,
and my sister. All of us living together, my grandpa, and all.
There's like ten people living under one roof. I let them know,
"Hey, I applied to all these places." And they were like, "Okay,
well, we've never heard of these schools but Cal State Fullerton
is down the street. We need help with the mortgage now. Think
what's best for you but do you want to go away?" Going away
wasn't something I thought about. If I really wanted to, I
could've left. As it is, I felt guilty. I felt like I was taking
advantage of my education. If I left, then I felt like I was
abandoning them. These universities to them were not practical,
"Okay, but seriously, what's the point?" I let the guilt get to me.
With them it was "Go to Cal State Fullerton." That was the main
thing. "Go down the street."

As for my friends, they were like, "Oh, you applied!" Thankfully being involved in Latina Leadership Network here on campus, my friends all pushed each other so much. Everyone has their story. They make you feel like, "Okay, it's achievable. You're worth it. You're gonna go." They were all wonderful and great. "Once you get accepted to all of them, then you can narrow down your pick. Don't worry about it. Keep going." I got support from friends, the campus community.

I was admitted to every university that I applied to. All the Cal States and all the UC's! I had initially decided on Cal State Fullerton. Where else am I going to go? It's perfect. It's local. But the deciding factor was what my friends in Latina Leadership, my adviser, and the Career Center, Janine, and my co-worker kept saying. Basically the campus community told me, well, Janine specifically in her office told me, "If you've been admitted to a UC. UC's like Berkeley and LA, you're gonna go there. Why are you thinking Cal State Fullerton?" Because forever, while attending community college, I always asked, "What's better, UC or Cal State? What's the difference?" It was always, "It depends on your major or program. I can't tell you to choose one." No, Janine and my people told me, "You're going to go to a university because it will make a difference when you shake someone's hand and you hand them a card and you tell them, 'Hi, I'm Dana. I go to Cal State Fullerton' or 'Hi, I'm Dana. I'm a student at Berkeley or I'm a student at UCLA.'"

I was like, "Okay, that sounds cool but where or how am I going to get there?" The next factor was, I eliminated my four Cal States, what university do I go to? Berkeley was just like, "Oh my God, I'm going to go to Berkeley. That's the one!"

When I am at the community college, it's like a dream world. The sky's the limit. When I get home, that's when the reality sinks in. This is my family. School is school but these are the people who I see. I can't leave them. How am I going to go to Berkeley? How am I going to help pay rent? Where am I going

to live? How am I going to eat? They need me and I need them.
I can't leave.

When I am at the community college, it's like a dream world.
The sky's the limit. When I get home, that's when the reality
sinks in. This is my family. School is school but these
are the people who I see. I can't leave them.

I found out about a UCLA van pool. My counselor told me,
"On Magnolia and Orangethorpe, I see a UCLA van pool. It
takes students straight there. I was like, "Okay, then UCLA is
the one because I can stay home. I can commute. It's still a
university. It's not as close as Cal State Fullerton, so I'm still
technically going out into the world." Even though LA is Orange
County's neighbor, I've never been to LA. To me, it was like a
whole new world. This big adventure. UCLA was the one
because Cal States weren't going to be an option for me. My
advisers and everyone made it clear, "You're gonna go to a
university. That's it." So I was like, "Okay, I'm worth it. I can do
this." They told me, "You got accepted for a reason." UC's were
it. Then UCLA was the one because I could still live at home, be
there for my family and get to live my university dream.

Irvine was close too. Another counselor was pushing for
Irvine because it's not that far. But UCLA was like, the name!
Obviously hearing the name UCLA, I felt like so, "Oh my God!"
UC Irvine, it wasn't as really well known. A part of me still
thinks, "Should I have gone to Irvine?"

I hadn't visited these campuses, even though I had gone on
the northern California trip. I had seen Berkeley, USC, but I
hadn't gone to UCLA or Irvine. When I was accepted, I didn't
even know where I was going. People told me, "UCLA has a
beautiful campus." I'm like, "Really?" I had no idea where I was
going. The name UCLA sounded amazing. My advisers told me,
"Try UCLA. I heard the departments are good." I got good

feedback. I felt I would make my family proud of me, people proud when I told people I transferred to UCLA. It was more of a name thing, a pride thing.

Once I got admitted and I knew I was gonna transfer, I felt amazing! I felt like, "Wow, everything I want is achievable! I felt like I accomplished the American Dream. Pull yourself up by your boot straps. It's all possible!" Especially being a Latina, who's low-income, who came from a single-parent household. It was a dream come true! I felt like I'm finally living the dream. So many in our community don't take advantage of the opportunities. I felt like this is it. This is it for me. More importantly, it's for my family and for my friends. It's so they could see it is possible. I felt like I was becoming a role model. Like I was becoming a leader.

Once I got to UCLA, the depression hit again. I felt so intimidated. Sitting in classes at community college is one thing. Some people raise their hands, some don't. The teachers are very welcoming. UCLA is like Darwinism. Survival of the fittest. The words that were coming out of people's mouths! These professors are there to challenge you. They're not there to nurture you and to help you grow.

Community college is a place where you have family. These people want to see you transfer. They're there for you. UCLA is a place where, we're going to get you out to the real world. You're going to be the best. If you're not cut out for it, then we're going to get rid of you here. I remember someone saying there's a difference between your papers you did in college and a UCLA "A" paper. I was terrified and intimidated by everyone around me.

Thankfully, still being attached to my community college people, I felt that's where I had my roots. Every time I felt I wasn't going to make it at UCLA, I would come back and talk to Dee from Latino Leadership or talk with my friends or talk to Janine. Talk with my supportive foundation. They were pushing me, helping, like "You need to finish your paper. You need to do this. You can do it."

A person having the belief in me that I didn't have for myself is what pushed me. It felt great transferring, saying where I'm going to go. Actually being there was a huge wake-up call. But all the challenges and all the intimidation has helped push me to a higher level.

> *A person having the belief in me that I didn't*
> *have for myself is what pushed me.*

The thinking it's brought out in my papers and in the way I analyze is something I wouldn't even have dreamed of before UCLA. The language in even a simple essay at UCLA. Who else talks like that? I notice I've grown. I go back and talk to my homies or old friends from high school and they're like, "Where the hell you'd get into? What word was that or what are you talking about?" I now have a world perspective. Community college helped me realize that it's not about my town or that town or this little city. There's more out there. UCLA has shown me a global perspective. It's been amazing!

I finished summer school last week, so being in summer school, I was like, "Oh my God, if I graduate next year it's going to be a miracle." Well, I got B's in my classes for summer school so my GPA is at 3.0. That's the lowest it has ever been in my life. I've gone into thinking, "Am I really worth this?" Again, this whole self-doubt. I came back to talk to my base people. I scheduled lunches. Been to see my adviser. Been to see my main mentors who helped shape me into what I am. They've all really pushed me. They told me, "You need to go to a Master's program and a Ph.D. This isn't it." I realized not only did I have the potential for community college, I am going to graduate from UCLA. I know that's for sure. They're not going to let me fail. I have the drive and coming from where I've come from,

I'm not going to let go of this. This is mine! I'm going to keep fighting for it.

Next is gonna be a Master's and a Ph.D. Exactly which program, I have no idea. I know I need to start with the research. I know I need to cut out all of my excuses. I'm the first one. There's so many Latinas here. Being in a community here where they're all pushing for you, they're all fighting for the same thing. My other friend is at USC. I even asked her, "How's it going or how can I help?" My other friend transferred to UC Davis with her children. I love seeing her story come out so beautifully. She's flourishing so much. It empowers me to believe in myself.

It's changing my life because in high school, I was just glad I didn't get pregnant. That was it. Going to a community college has made me grow so much. Then transferring shows me I can do it.

It's changing my life because in high school,
I was just glad I didn't get pregnant. That was it.
Going to a community college has made me grow so much.
Then transferring shows me I can do it.

There are people sitting in their Range Rovers while I'm sitting on the bus on the 920 in Los Angeles, hoping I don't get shot on the way to UCLA. It makes me appreciate everything so much more. I realize that there's not that great of a difference between what's in your mind and mine. I can use my thinking abilities, my analytical skills, my brain skills, my people skills, all these skills that I'm filled with because of college, that have prepared me for my future careers. I can use that. I can make it. I don't have to be a sad story. I can make it something positive.

Next is gonna be another degree. Something where I'm able to give back to the community. I've stayed grounded in my roots, stayed with my family. My advisers, especially Dee from Latina Leadership, have made me realize that it's beautiful that

I've stayed so connected but it's time to go. Time to move on. Time to write my next chapter, really develop myself on another level, not just being at home with the family.

I have learned from failure. My first quarter at UCLA, I failed a class. I got a C minus. Because of that minus, I had to retake the class. I took it hard because it was the first time I had ever failed a class. To me, C minus was like, "Okay, I passed," but over there, that's failing. That's it. That's where I really got an awakening. This isn't gonna to be smooth sailing. You're gonna have to work for this. Because of that failure, I've been pushing myself more. I've been growing more. I've found my potential. I found the drive. The need to actually succeed. If it wasn't for that failure, then I wouldn't have been able to push myself as a writer.

You get in a comfort level in your writing. That failure helped me realize like, "Okay, you're at UCLA writing like a little girl. You need to start thinking like these fellow geniuses around you." I have students who are authors in my classes. I've Googled them. I'm not going to lie. I've seen how much their books are selling on Amazon and all these bookstores. I'm like, "Well, if they can do it and I'm in the same class, maybe I can do it." I've been pushing my writing level, so failure definitely serves as a wake-up call. Because of my negativity and self-doubt, it could have easily ended there. Because I have such a great support group academically, they really made me try. Try the best I can.

To really be successful, you need drive. You need to have the drive, the will to do it. Also, family. Family's been key. They haven't been there to give me the advice, but they've been there to support me. I've made it clear to them why I'm doing it. Understanding my desires has made them want to support me. They're all Bruins fans now in blue and gold. It's beautiful, showing pride. So my drive, my family, academic support from my mentors and the community from where I come from.

People here at my community college, specifically because whenever I'm not able to believe in myself, they've always been there to catch me. Always been there to support me 100%. They instill a belief in me that needs to be there. Drive, family, and mentors to help you. That's it I think.

Family's been key. They haven't been there to give me
the advice, but they've been there to support me.
I've made it clear to them why I'm doing it.
Understanding my desires has made them want to support me.
They're all Bruins fans now in blue and gold.

If you want it, you can get it. My grandpa has this saying, *los que pueden, no quieren y los que quieren no pueden* [literal translation: those that can, don't want to and those that want to, can't]. But me, I'm fortunate, I want it and I can do it. I'm gonna do it. Whereas I see others around me who have the opportunities and they don't try. They don't want it. It's sad. I'm glad I have it. I've surrounded myself with a very positive environment. All strong women. Most of them Latinas who have pushed me to where I am. Being around people who have made it has helped me.

If I had to do it over again, I would have applied to USC. I wouldn't have been so scared. I would've applied. Applied. That's it. I applied where I did but sometimes I wonder. I don't know if it's true, but I've been told, Berkeley and UCLA are harder to get into than USC. I know I could've gotten in. I would've applied but I think UCLA was the best choice for me, the best fit. It's farther, geographically, than USC. So I've been exposed to more of the world.

I've seen things on my daily ride on the bus, which I've seen on TMZ. Where I come from, they think that is cool. We like celebrities and stuff. People think that's cool. I've seen the Hollywood sign. Just the adventure has been phenomenal though. The professors have been incredible. The campus, every time I walk onto campus, I get a sense of overwhelming pride. I don't know if everyone who lives at UCLA can say that or so near the campus can. After riding a bus for 2 ½ hours through LA? Hell yeah! I'm proud when I get to campus! It's safe. That's where I'm gonna grow.

I would've applied to USC if I could do things differently but in the end, UCLA was the best for me. For the book festival there, I took my niece to campus. Now she's dreaming of college. I have other little teenage friends and cousins. They're all getting into gang-related activity. It sucks! I've taken them to campus. They're amazed, "Oh my gosh, this is really cool. Oh my gosh, look at those women." Even if it's just the chicks there or the sports or the campus, I'm glad they're thinking of college. Because in my little group, we could easily name so many people who are locked up at the LAC or WASCO or all these prisons, but it's so difficult to name someone who's at a university. Being that role model, being at a UC, I think was the best choice.

Because in my little group, we could easily name
so many people who are locked up at the
LAC or WASCO or all these prisons,
but it's so difficult to name someone who's at a university.

Thankfully because of the Latina Leadership Network, I come back through the years. I have that little support network. It helps so much! We talked about when it's time to apply, everyone's fears. Where do you want to apply? What are you scared of? Being able to share my story, I feel like I've been able to inspire and let those girls know that you need to apply. Who cares if you get in or where you get in? Just apply! We share our fears. We need to have that network. It's nice that you can talk to someone who's in your same shoes and knows what you're going through.

In transferring from the community college, there's so much more to it but I think the key things that stood out were the mental struggles I went through. Not academically because academically I was fine, I was doing my job. It was so emotional. That's where the difficulty was, being Latina, being low-income. So many barriers were restricting me. The way I was able to get over those was simply by having people there who told me, "You can do it." It knocked down all my worries. It's crazy how easy it is. I made it worse in my mind that it actually was. Transferring, it's not that difficult. Maybe some people might argue.

That's where the difficulty was, being Latina, being low-income. So many barriers were restricting me. The way I was able to get over those was simply by having people there who told me, "You could do it." It knocked down all my worries. It's crazy how easy it is.

Transfer-wise, when it comes down to the tangible stuff, it's very simple. Filling out the application online, there are fee waivers. I thought I didn't qualify for a fee waiver. I called one of my advisers at EOPS. They had the fee waiver ready for me. It was so simple. Go online, fill out the stuff, send out your transcripts. If you've been doing what you had to do, it's all very simple. Follow IGETC. That's it. That's all it took! All of the emotional stuff is what holds people back when it comes to school. Their children, their family, their self-doubt. When it comes down to the tangible stuff, it's so easy. Really, there's nothing to it!

Something else that might be helpful for transfer students, I would have liked to have been more informed when I was at community college about the benefits transfer students get. I wanted to stay home but I didn't know that we were guaranteed housing if we did transfer. I didn't know about that. I don't know why. I wish I would've had more guidance in the aspect of the benefits I was gonna get as a transfer student. You're a junior so you get this amount, you get guaranteed housing or you get this and that.

And then most importantly, people need to remember to keep their network and their contacts really close. Those have played such a huge role for me. Even though, emotionally, it's not my best friends who guided me from high school, these new networks and these new contacts I've made at the college campus pushed me to transfer and have continued to keep me going. It's different for other people who live on campus because they're able to access their resources.

Being a woman, it's hard because society depends on us so much. We're given so much more responsibility. Our social conventions are, they say, the man wears the pants in the house. Well for Latinas, yeah, the man wears the pants, but the Latinas choose it. We women are the ones who run the house. We run everything. For Latinas it's so much more difficult than the average woman because we have our social conventions of what we're supposed to fulfill, our certain rules. Then we have our cultural conventions also, playing such a huge impact. I hope other Latinas realize, do it for your family and do it for everyone else in your community, but most importantly, do it for you. You deserve it! You don't have to feel guilty for leaving everyone behind because in the end, it's best for everyone else.

Profile update: Dana transferred to the University of California, Los Angeles where she graduated with her Bachelor of Arts Degree in English. She went on to earn her teacher credential in Secondary Education from the California State University, Fullerton. She now teaches English to high school students in Southern California.

Chapter Nine

Sacrifice This Now and Have That Later

I knew I was going to go to college ever since I was in elementary school. I always talked about it. I'm not sure if it was the TV shows that I watched or what. The shows would have people that were smart and they went to college. People would tell me I was smart, so I knew I was going to go to college. My sisters weren't in college yet. I've always been really into school. At least, at the time, in elementary I was really into school. I got good grades. I'm not sure if my teachers spoke to me about it but I always knew that I was going to go to college.

I'm not sure if I knew that I would get a successful career out of it but I remember always talking about it. I'm going to go to the university after high school. I didn't know any universities but I always knew that I was going to go to college. That's how I remembered it. I always wanted to be a teacher. When I was in second grade, I wanted to teach second grade. When I was in third, I wanted to teach third.

I thought college was like regular school, like what I was already doing. I didn't even know that it cost money, because I went to public school. I didn't know the amount of work would be more difficult. I thought that after 12th I go to 13 and 14, it was automatic.

I would honestly have to say my family was absent in my planning for college, if I'm going to be brutally honest. They would support me by asking me things but that's about it.

I had two sisters that were going to community college part-time, so I saw that but I didn't really see that college was their life, like how it was for me when I started going. It took up so much of my time and they worked full-time.

When it came to the community college application, I had an older friend help me with it. When it came to financial aid, my friend's boyfriend helped me with it. When it came to the BOG Fee Waiver, it was through a friend. Everything with friends. My family would sometimes ask a few little questions, here and there, about the placement tests or something. I remember going to my sisters about it. But they weren't so passionate about it, so I don't think I saw them as a resource.

I didn't have a car, so my dad would drop me off after he got out of work for my evening classes. He wanted me to go to college but I don't think he knew that it cost money.

I didn't have a car, so my dad would drop me off after he got out of work for my evening classes. He wanted me to go to college but I don't think he knew that it cost money. But he would ask me about it. You could tell he liked that I was going to school. He just wasn't knowledgeable in that area. He helped me in the little ways that he could, by dropping me off or not complaining like, "What? You have a class at 8 o'clock?! You're not going." He wasn't like that at all. He wouldn't get in my way with studying time. He helped me in ways that he felt that he could.

I didn't feel like it had to be a conversation. I felt like going to college was my decision. I didn't really think that they would understand. He would ask me about stuff about me being a teacher cuz that's what I was going to be, a teacher.

I had a friend and we would take every class together. My dad would even pick her up because she didn't have a car either.

I had a friend and we would take every class together. My dad would even pick her up because she didn't have a car either. That's really nice. I look back and I don't feel like there are that many parents that would do that for college students. Especially when they get up at four in the morning to go to work. Then get out, hurry, take me and my friend to campus.

Then a year later, he bought me a car. If it wasn't for my car, then that could have been a reason why I would have been delayed in getting my education. The car helped with going to college. The fact that he bought it for me. I didn't have to pay for it. He got it for me.

I'll never forget that day! It was a brand new truck! I thought it was for him. He said, "Here, so you can go to school." I was like, "What?!" My sister was like, "What?!" I used to always joke with him like, "I need a car, dad." One day he forgot to pick me up from work. He would even take me to work! He would take me everywhere! He came home one day with a brand new truck. I was like, "Aww, you deserve it, dad. You work so hard." I said, "Okay, I'm going to drive the little, old car." He handed me the keys to the new truck! It made me feel like he wanted me to go the right way. By doing something like that. I think that's huge! Especially because my family doesn't have the money to be like, "I'm going to buy my daughter a car." That's not really us.

Coming to community college and my first impression, I had culture shock! I graduated from a small high school where the population was 95% Hispanic. Here there were Asians, whites, Middle-easterners, etc. Huge culture shock! People wearing sandals when it rained, the rainbow of colors.

Coming to community college and my first impression, I had culture shock! I graduated from a small high school where the population was 95% Hispanic. Here there were Asians, whites, Middle-easterners, etc. Huge culture shock! People wearing sandals when it rained, the rainbow of colors. Different clothing. I wasn't exposed to that before. Different music. It was all different.

In the beginning, it was different. I wasn't really sure how to approach people in my classes. The amount of people was a little overwhelming as well. But I got comfortable really fast.

In class, if there was something that I was knowledgeable about, I've always been the type of student that participates and talks a lot. I didn't really have a problem with that.

But in the beginning, I remember feeling really overwhelmed by the workload because I didn't feel that my high school classes prepared me for the work that I was going to get here. That's for sure! Especially because I was a C student in high school, barely making C's, so to come here, I mean, trying to get a C here, it wasn't the same as high school. I wasn't prepared for it. I remember being so overwhelmed that sometimes I felt like I wanted to throw up when it came to writing a paper. I didn't feel like I could write at the college level.

I remember being so overwhelmed that sometimes I felt like I wanted to throw up when it came to writing a paper. I didn't feel like I could write at the college level.

I remember the first big paper I wrote was for an art class. When the professor handed it back she said, "I'm going to give you a chance to do it again" because it was that bad. She said, "You got a D on the paper, but I'm going to give you a chance to do it again."

I was so overwhelmed that I wanted to throw up. I had an anxiety attack because I was so stressed out. But it was never an option to stop. That was never an option.

I asked for help. I have an aunt, she's American and she's really into photography and art. I called her. She's also an elementary teacher. I asked her for help with my paper. Plus, my older friend, helped me revise my paper. At that time I wasn't aware of the resources I had at the Learning Resource Center. That I could go there. I looked for outside sources. The second time, I got a B on my paper.

Once I started taking remedial English classes, the professor introduced me to different tools at the college. I started using the Writing Center to help me. When I had problems, they would see that I had gone to the Writing Center, so that would help. They knew I was trying. I struggled with my writing in the beginning. I didn't know how to write or site.

*Once I started taking remedial English classes,
the professor introduced me to different tools at the college.
I started using the Writing Center to help me.*

Things changed for me my last semester here because I had to start working more. At first, I worked at a youth center. It was just a few hours. I kept working cuz I could get hours plus my dad had to refinance the house. The mortgage went up so then I had to start paying rent. Things changed for me. I got a job at IHOP. I started going to school in the evening. I wasn't happy about it at all cuz I didn't want to go to school in the evening. I wanted to go to school with all the young people. I was not happy about that at all. It made me feel like my family didn't support what I was doing. I look back now. I feel like that was really selfish of me. I could do both, you know? I did it.

My sister told me, "I've been paying rent. You need to start paying rent. You need to do this. You can go to school in the evening. Everyone does it." I had a fit! I wasn't happy. I did it anyway. I started going to school in the evening. I started to get a little bit more tired. I didn't have the time for myself that I was used to. For my friends, for my social life. I adjusted to it. I actually liked it even better because I wasn't annoyed by the text messages and students talking in the evening. It would really annoy me during the day classes, all the talking. A lot of people were there that didn't really want to be there in classes during the day.

That was my last semester in community college. It was spring. It made me mature a little bit more having to do that. I did feel upset about it, but never to the point where it was going to discourage me especially cuz I was that close to transfer.

I took 12 units that semester. I always wrote down the classes that I needed left in advance. I always knew what I was going to take. For me, I was very organized. I like to write down my plan. Anything that I could cross off, a class or anything, I loved to do that!

I knew I was going to have to transfer pretty soon. I wasn't aware of deadlines so much, like November 30th for the UC's and CSU's. My friend worked at the Transfer Center. She told me, "I'm going to get ready to transfer." I said "I think me too." And she said "It's okay, they'll take you. You've already completed your Golden Four. Take this in the summer. You'll be good." I started calculating my GPA. And she actually helped me with my CSU application.

Going to community college is that hardest part about getting your Bachelor's Degree. I can see why people don't make it. If your will is not strong enough or they don't even know what their major is or if the passion is not there, then they give up.

I had been waiting for this moment the whole time! Three years here at community college. That's the hardest part in higher education, if you go to community college. I don't know what it is to go for four years at the university but I think community college is the hardest part. Especially because you are taking classes that you already took in high school. Classes that you don't want to take. Classes that you don't like. Going to community college is that hardest part about getting your Bachelor's Degree. I can see why people don't make it. If your will is not strong enough or they don't even know what their major is or if the passion is not there, then they give up.

When it came to applying to transfer, I was so excited! I had been waiting for that moment. I didn't care how long it took me at Cal State Fullerton, but I wanted to get out of community college. It was really tiring.

Something else I remember that was negative was that my sisters were going to community college as well, but they would go part-time. I felt deep down inside, although I know they wished me the best, it was hard for them to see that I was going to a university before them. My oldest sister is 9 years older than me. And then, my other sister is 6 years older than me so that's a huge gap. When I would talk to them, I didn't really feel like I got the reaction that I expected. They went to the graduations and stuff but not so much like I expected. I had to remind myself, I'm doing this for me. Nobody else. I have to keep going.

They went to the graduations and stuff but not so much like I expected. I had to remind myself, I'm doing this for me. Nobody else. I have to keep going.

I have always known the steps to transfer from the community college because I took a Career/Life Planning class. I gained a lot of knowledge from that class. Even before that, I would always take the initiative to do my own research. Also, I would meet with counselors to be on the safe side.

I've always been really passionate about higher education. I'm not sure what it was. The autonomy that came with it? I always liked to search and become more knowledgeable so I can share the resources with my friends.

From the moment that I got here, I always came to the Transfer Center to get my major prep sheet. I would follow the Cal State Fullerton requirements. I always knew I would go to Cal

State Fullerton because it's the local school. I was paying rent at home so there's no way I was going to leave my house. I couldn't and I didn't feel that I wanted to. Cal State Fullerton seemed like the right choice.

I did apply to other schools. I applied to Cal State Dominguez Hills, to Cal State Long Beach and Pomona and San Diego. That was it. The only reason that I did it was because I got the application fee waived. I had choices. I wanted to see if I could get in. I wondered if they would accept me. They all did! Deep down inside I felt it might be nice if I could move to San Diego. But no. I didn't even know where Cal State Dominguez Hills was located. It's not that far.

The only reason that I did it was because I got the application fee waived. I had choices. I wanted to see if I could get in. I wondered if they would accept me. They all did!

I felt obligated to stay at home because of rent. And then I was happy living at home. I didn't feel like my dad got in my way. I had a very good social life. I was very social. My friends were very important at that time. They were a big priority. Then I had a boyfriend too. So I felt happy where I was. I didn't feel like I had to go anywhere else.

When I got admitted to the universities, I felt like, "Oh my gosh, I making it! I'm doing it!" I felt really, really, good about myself. I felt like I accomplished something really good. To me, I felt the community college experience is a little more challenging than Cal State Fullerton. Community college is not as expensive so it doesn't hurt that much to stop.

To this day, I have in my room my Associate's Degree in a frame and my Bachelor's Degree side by side. To me, it means so much more when I look at my Associate's. I remember how hard I worked. How challenging it was.

*To this day, I have in my room my Associate's Degree
in a frame and my Bachelor's Degree side by side.
To me, it means so much more when I look at my Associate's.
I remember how hard I worked. How challenging it was.*

Applying to transfer, I felt like I was going to have a really good career now. I was going to be successful. I'm this young and I'm going to get my Bachelor's in a few years. I might as well go all the way and get my Masters. Doctorate even. It made me feel like I can do more because I felt like I was really young. Why stop there if I can overcome this much?

I don't think any single one experience helped me. Perhaps seeing how hard my parents worked at factories. My dad has been a machine operator, getting such a low pay after he's been working there for 30 years struggling. Then once my mom's company moved, she was never able to get a stable job.

Living paycheck to paycheck, it was really hard. It was harder when I was in high school, then it was when I was a child. I didn't want to live like that. I wanted to live a comfortable life.

At that time I felt like I wanted to be a teacher. I felt really passionate about it so I knew I couldn't go to vocational school to get my teaching credential. I had to go to college, a university.

It's not so much experience that you need to be a success. It's my personal characteristics that got me to where I am because I'm very dedicated. I'm very driven. When I feel passion about something, I give it my all.

The most important thing to be a successful transfer student is finding out what you're passionate about because coming here as an undeclared major, as a Latina, that's really difficult and it makes you feel like you don't have a purpose. It makes you feel like, "Oh, I'll think about my major and when I find it then I'll start going to school." It's really important to feel like you have a reason or purpose.

Another really important lesson is learning how to delay

gratification. When you're in school, when you're not really working, it's really hard when you see people that are working at their office jobs, having money, having a car, friends going out to dinner, shopping. They're not big luxuries, but at that age, you want those things. You wanna have that lifestyle and even going out. It all costs money. That's something that's really important. You have to remind yourself, "Not now. I have to sacrifice this now and have that later." That's really important because I remember it was discouraging when I would see I'm going to school but I feel like I have nothing. I would see my friends, they seemed really comfortable and happy. It was discouraging. I had to remind myself, "I can't. I can't." Even going to school and opening three credit cards. That's not really delaying gratification because you're charging and at the end you're going to get in debt. You'll end up leaving school so you can get more work hours to pay the credit cards. That's a really important lesson.

Another tip for success is being focused and learning how to prioritize. Surround yourself with the right people. Because at that age, you think that your relationship is so much that it can last. You wanna dedicate so much time to it. It could last. I've been with my boyfriend since that time but surrounding yourself with the right people is critical. If you have a boyfriend and he's not really into your goals or not really into education, he's not going to understand. He's going to be like, "Oh, you have to study again? Or don't go to class." It's going to bring you down. So you're going to be like, "You're right, I should be with you more. I shouldn't go to school now. I can finish when I'm 30."

If you have a boyfriend and he's not really into your goals or not really into education, he's not going to understand. He's going to be like, "Oh, you have to study again? Or don't go to class." It's going to bring you down.

Something else to think about, your friends are like, "Come on! Let's go out." They do pressure you and you do care. You do want to keep up with everybody and everything that they're doing. Prioritizing and letting them know, "Don't take it personal but this is something that's really important to me. We can't go to lunch tomorrow. I can't go today." This is really important. They have to care about it. And if they don't, then you need to learn how to deal with that situation. I remember my boyfriend wasn't going to school. He started working full-time. But he did give me that space. He knew that this was a huge priority. Probably my first priority. He was the first one in his family to graduate from high school, so the fact that I was here and I was so close to transferring, he thought that it was so huge. He really loved that about me. That's really important.

If I had to do it all over again. I don't think I would change anything because I feel like I was always on track. I had to take remedial classes. That's why it took me 3 years. I made up for it by going to summer school and doing winter session. I was always on it. I took Saturday classes, if I had to, even if that meant I can't go out Friday night. It's the life that I chose.

I'm very proud of myself because I look back and I am glad. How did I not get distracted? I had my friends that would go out Thursday, Friday, Saturday, and Sunday. They would go to shows. I would be like, "What?" I didn't even know what the transition from day to night was like because I was always in school. That's something that I really appreciate now. I like to sit outside and see the sun go down. I was indoors for whole days and nights! I really don't think I would do anything different.

I didn't even know what the transition from day to night was like because I was always in school. That's something that I really appreciate now. I like to sit outside and see the sun go down. I was indoors for whole days and nights!

My first year was the hardest, because I didn't have a car. I was overwhelmed with the work load. I handled it the best I could. I could've been like, "I'm going to wait until I get a car. I can't do this." I had a class at nine in the morning and at one in the afternoon. I would stay on campus all day. I would get so frustrated and bored. I would say if I had a car I could sleep, go to the mall...

Something that really discouraged my transfer was my major. Originally, I wanted to be a political science major. I was gonna get my credential in social science so I could teach economics and government. I was so on it all the time with my classes. One time I met with a counselor. She explained to me that I needed to take an extra thirteen units of history, of geography, of all these social sciences or I could pass the social science test for the credential. I had been reading about the credential exam. I heard that that test was almost impossible to pass. Most people took the extra classes. I thought I am not going to do this. This is stupid! I've been on it. I'm not going to spend another year here. I started to do it anyway but when I transferred, I changed my major. I remember finding out that I still had a lot of classes when I thought I was so done. It was so discouraging for me. The information about the classes was accurate. I just didn't know. I didn't know there were so many pre-requisites to get into the credential program. It was that extensive. I didn't know.

I was so mad that day! I was angry! All day I was angry, I kept venting to everyone. I was so mad, "Why?! Why did they do this, why? It's so stupid!"

Even so, I had to do it. That's the way I felt. I felt so passionate about education. That's what I wanted to teach. It's what I had to do, so I needed to shut up.

That's why I decided to pursue higher education because I feel so determined. I get so much energy from it! I can't even explain it! I love to encourage people to pursue post-secondary education.

*That's why I decided to pursue higher education because
I feel so determined. I get so much energy from it!
I can't even explain it! I love to encourage people
to pursue post-secondary education.*

Something that can really help students, is knowing that other people are on the same page. That you're not the only one facing these educational barriers. Maybe you're a straight A student but your parents don't understand that you have to be at your friend's house until midnight or pull an all-nighter because you have to study. Because in our culture that's not the way it works, "What do you mean you're going to be at the library until ten? The library closes early." That's not true because they don't know. It really helps to share problems.

I remember I took the Chicano studies course. Hearing Professor Adela Lopez talk about her experience, that she had a really hard time when her mom because she wouldn't believe her when she said she was going to the library and had to be there until it closed. Her mother didn't believe that the library closed that late. I remember feeling I can relate to that and feeling like everyone else in that class could too. It makes you feel like, "Okay, I'm not the only one. College is for me. Everyone is doing it. We all find our own ways." Knowing that other people are on the same page, culturally, I think that's huge!

*When you know your family is not supportive of your
education, it feels really bad. It can be discouraging, but when
you see it from a cultural point of view, you understand.*

When you know your family is not supportive of your education, it feels really bad. It can be discouraging, but when you see it from a cultural point of view, you understand, "Oh, it's not that they don't want to. It's that they don't understand. They don't know." That lifts your spirits and it makes you feel "Okay,

I can keep doing this. I'm not the only one. I'll figure it out until they can understand." That's really big.

Profile update: Jaqueline transferred to the California State University, Fullerton and graduated with her Bachelor of Science Degree in Human Services. She then continued her education and graduated with her Master of Science Degree in Counseling - Student Development in Higher Education from Long Beach State University. She now works as an academic advisor and counselor at a community college and at the California State University, Fullerton.

Chapter Ten
Go Big or Go Home

My freshmen year in high school, I was in the AVID program which is a program for high school students to learn about college and to plan that out. For me, at that time, I didn't really envision myself in college because that's something that my parents didn't talk about at home. They encouraged me to go to school but not to go to college. I envisioned college as a goal that I could possibly get to, but I didn't really feel the connection in that program. I didn't feel connected. I didn't feel like it was for me. I felt it was for people that have the information already and have people in their lives that can walk them through it. I didn't have people like that at home. It made me feel subconsciously, hopeful that I could get there, but I didn't feel I had the support I needed to get there, even though I did have teachers who encouraged me to go to college. My family wanted to be there but didn't know how, so I felt disconnected from the whole college experience in high school.

For me, at that time, I didn't really envision myself in college because that's something that my parents didn't talk about at home.

My senior year of high school, I realized I had two options: either work full-time, which I ended up doing anyway, or do something with my life. There wasn't a specific moment. I didn't think about it. I just did it. Once I came to the college campus, I felt very overwhelmed. I didn't know where to start but I knew I had to. It was already in me to go for it.

After I graduated from high school, I went to work full-time, right when I turned 18. I started coming to community college right away too. I started with 5 classes but I would drop some, so I would end up with one class. That whole year, actually, for two or three years, I was completely lost.

Completely lost. I remember Vince from the Transfer Center coming into one of my Sociology classes. It was that semester, the first or the second. He was talking about all these resources at the Transfer Center and blah blah blah, but I felt everybody already knew way more than I did about the transfer process. It seemed everybody already knew more than me about how to transfer. Students and professors.

Maybe it was because of how I was living my life at the time. It was always on the go and thinking about what's next. Getting ready for the unexpected. I perceived people here to be that way too. I didn't feel connected once again. I remember Vince saying, "Come visit the Transfer Center." I came one time with Dolores and I felt uncomfortable. I didn't feel comfortable talking about my story as an illegal immigrant and about being an undocumented student because I had all these issues that I was dealing with: financial issues, identity issues, family issues and all these other issues that overwhelmed me. I didn't know how to open up to people here so that they could help me. I felt completely lost. I didn't know where to begin.

I didn't feel comfortable talking about my story as an illegal immigrant and about being an undocumented student because I had all these issues that I was dealing with: financial issues, identity issues, family issues and all these other issues that overwhelmed me. I didn't know how to open up to people here so that they could help me.

I remember telling my dad, "I'm going to go find out if I can go to college. I am going to try to find something, anything, for an undocumented student." Because we didn't have any information available. I mean, I never even heard of the Dream Act or AB540 before coming to college. I didn't even know about the law and the policy. I felt determined to find out, to find some sort of break, some way. I thought, "Where there's a will, there's a way."

I always told my dad that my situation, my lack of a social security number, was not going to determine my character, my integrity. I went to see if I could find out some information so I could go to college. And sure enough, I came to the Admissions and Records Office. They gave me the information I needed to enroll.

I always told my dad that my situation,
my lack of a social security number,
was not going to determine my character, my integrity.

I did not ask my dad for permission to go to community college. No. It was more like, "Hey dad, I'm going to go down to the college and see what I can find out." Then I came home and told my dad, "This is what happened." As I was finding out more information, I would go back and report. He'd be like, "Okay, mija, its good."

But as far as planning, no planning. My dad doesn't know the system. He did not attend college, so he did not know how to be a resource for me, to help me navigate it.

When I first came to community college, I felt excited! I felt like, "Oh, man! I don't even know if I'm supposed to be here! I don't even know if I can pay any tuition." I knew it was going to be $150 per unit, only because I did not have knowledge of the AB540 in-state tuition exemption. Without that, I wasn't even going to be able to get through it. I was going to be coming and wasting my time, which I did end up doing for two or three years. I remember coming on campus and saying to myself, "This is college! This is a college campus!"

When I first came to community college, I felt excited! I felt like, "Oh, man! I don't even know if I'm supposed to be here!"

At first, I didn't think I was gonna transfer. Maybe subconsciously, I thought, with persistence, "Hey Thalia, you can do it!" But I didn't plan for it. I literally took it one step at a time. Sometimes I felt I was behind when I was actually ahead.

Walking around campus, getting to know the facilities and people, I felt excited! I felt like, "Wow! This is college!" Then in the back of my head I thought, "Well, this is kind of like an extension of high school." Still, I felt excited. Walking on campus, getting my books, I remember going to the bookstore. I thought, "Man, its expensive! How am I going to get through this? I need to work more hours." I was also paying for my sister's tuition and my tuition at the same time. I was thinking, "How am I going to do it?"

My first negative experience was when I first went to talk to a counselor, who shall go un-named, across the street. I had already been here a few semesters. I was thinking, "Okay, well, I need to go see somebody because I'm taking a lot of classes now." I was completely lost again. I had a good semester, my grades were improving. I thought, "Well, it's gonna show. I didn't do so well here but I'm showing some progress now." I remember telling the counselor, "I want to go to a UC." He was like, "UC's don't take people with W's, so here's a Cal State." The counselor said, "UC's don't take people with W's. Maybe Cal State Fullerton, Cal State Long Beach." I thought "Okay, well, thank you." That was across the street, a year and a half ago. That totally devastated me! I thought, "Okay, then. I will work towards Cal States." At that moment, because of what he's telling me, he's a professional, he knows. I made the decision as a transfer student to transfer to Cal State Fullerton because of him.

I was working towards that idea. I had decided on a major. Then it was around the time my friend, Miguel, applied to UC Irvine. I applied to Cal State Fullerton at the time. I was like, "Okay, I'm going to transfer to Cal State Fullerton." I made up my mind. That same semester, I was pretty bummed out, especially when my friend got the acceptance letter from UC Irvine. I got denied because I did not pay the fee for the application. I hadn't researched it or anything of that nature. That semester, I remember I was feeling very, very down. Super down! I thought about dropping out because of finances and because of the lack of support, my insecurities, not having the information about transferring. I wasn't putting myself out there. Instead of finding solutions, I was dwelling on a problem.

I remember talking to a friend and venting and talking to other people on campus. I had this one friend who I talked to every time we got out of class. I expressed all those insecurities to him. I felt supported when he listened. I'd go with him to the Transfer Center. He'd be like, "Thalia, you have good grades. You show that you're improving. You need to go big or go home, Thalia. You need to go big or go home!" Then he goes, "There's UCLA. The rep is coming." There were bulletin boards outside the Transfer Center with the schedule of visiting college representatives. He's like, "Go make an appointment, Thalia." and I was like, "No, no. No, I'm already going to apply to Cal State Fullerton. I'm already working towards that." It was the year before. I hadn't even applied to UCLA that time. It seemed impossible. "Thalia, just go. Just go, just go!" "Okay!" So I came in and I made an appointment.

After that conversation, I made the appointment. I was scheduled to see Casey from UCLA. Right away, I could tell he was so warm. I told him I was an undocumented student. I qualified for the AB540 exemption. Casey was really excited to tell me about all the resources available for students like myself. I remember just sitting there saying, "I want to maybe go to UCLA." He's like, "Oh, great!" He was excited by the situation I was in with me being an undocumented immigrant. I could not believe it! "What? Really?" Then I was super excited!

The fact that he knew what it was. He didn't label me or
stereotype me. That made me feel really, really good.
It made me feel safe in that environment.
I felt safe talking to him about my situation.

The fact that he knew what it was. He didn't label me or stereotype me. That made me feel really, really good. It made me feel safe in that environment. I felt safe talking to him about my situation. He told me about SITE. He told me about the McNair research program. He told me about the scholars program. He told me about the AAP Program over there.

He wrote everything down on my transcript. I remember telling him, "Well, I'm working towards Sociology at Cal State Fullerton but I am also looking at UCLA. I want to do Sociology." He told me about having to take Calculus. He told me, "It's going to set you back three semesters." Because I had to take a pre-Algebra course and then I had to take Calculus A and Calculus B. That was going to set me back at least a semester. I was like, "No, I'm not going to do Sociology then. What other programs can I get into? I really want to go to this school and have the experience." I don't even know why. He's like, "Well, what about Ethnic Studies? Are you interested?" I had taken all these general Ethnic Studies courses. I was like, "I love those classes! I love African-American Studies, Chicano Studies, and Women Studies. It deals with gender stuff, location, and social stratification and all that stuff." He told me, "Okay, this is what you need to do." He wrote everything on my piece of paper. I remember, because I felt so comfortable in his office. I felt accepted. I felt encouraged by my situation. I looked at him and said, "I can do this!" Because he believed in me. Especially because he's from UCLA. I was able to believe in myself versus that other guy, who's like "No!" Also, because I could relate to him. He looked at my transcript and he said, "I've been in your situation. I had W's. But look at you! You got a 4.0 GPA this semester. You're doing really well! Make sure you go to the Honors Program." He wrote everything down for me.

I felt so comfortable in his office. I felt accepted.
I felt encouraged by my situation. I looked at him and said,
"I can do this!" Because he believed in me. Especially because
he's from UCLA. I was able to believe in myself
versus that other guy, who's like "No!"

After that meeting, I remember going to the library. I felt like, "Okay, I have this information. What am I going to do with it?" I was like, "Okay, I'll take it one step at a time." Go to the counter, right? I checked out a laptop. Then I went upstairs. I remember this, and then I started working on a to-do list. All the things that he gave me, I rewrote them. It made me feel like I was doing something about it, even though I wasn't researching about it yet, but I was doing something. I felt empowered. I wasn't just, "Okay, I'm going to put it away. I'll go back to it later." I was seeking to do, to develop a plan on my own. I had already been here a very long time. All my friends were transferring to UC's. I was thinking I'm stuck. I don't want to be stuck. He told me about IDEAS at UCLA. It was a support system for undocumented students. I went and I researched all the stuff that was on that transcript. I made a to-do list with questions I had for later. And that's where it all began.

I was seeking to do, to develop a plan on my own.
I had already been here a very long time.
All my friends were transferring to UC's.
I was thinking I'm stuck. I don't want to be stuck.

Thankfully I had friends that were already transferring. When they were applying and I applied that first year, I felt lost. I didn't know where to begin. I was so afraid, because I was supposed to know what I was doing. That's when I thought, "I'm supposed to know this. I've been here for a while. I took a Career/Life Planning class. I'm supposed to know this!" But I didn't know it. I went to the Transfer Center more after that meeting with Casey.

Thankfully by the time it was my turn to complete the college applications the second time, I had reached out to more people. I felt comfortable asking for help when I didn't know something. When I looked at the screen, I felt comfortable with it because I had already been around the application process the year before. I felt okay. Last time, I didn't inform myself enough prior to applying. I did not have enough information to give me a sense of empowerment. The second time around, when I was looking at the online application, it was one step at a time. If I had any questions, I had people here who were willing to help me. They're here for that. They wanted me to succeed. I felt pretty good. Whenever I didn't know what the computer was asking, then I'd be like, "John! Help me!" Every time.

When it came time to choose where to apply to, it was UC Irvine because of the Sociology program there. That was a winner there. It was local. The deciding factor was commuting. The commute was the deciding factor because I thought back then that it wasn't possible to live on campus, but now I know that it is possible to live on campus.

As far as private universities, I was supposed to apply to Chapman University but I didn't because I remember walking on campus on a fieldtrip through the Transfer Center. I went to UCLA, UC Irvine. I went to San Diego, up north, and I went to Chapman University, Cal State Fullerton and Long Beach. When I walked on campus, on Chapman's campus, there was no diversity. No diversity that I could connect to. To me, it was too organized. It was too neat and organized. That was why I didn't apply. I had letters of recommendation. I had already started filling out the application online. Then I thought to myself, "Why am I doing this? Am I doing this because my sister's doing it or am I doing it because I really want to go there? Even if I did get money, would I fit in?" College is not just about getting the degree, it's about the experience. I mean, to me it is, anyway.

> *College is not just about getting the degree,*
> *it's about the experience.*

When I walked on the UCLA campus, the architecture and the grass and the stairs. It was all visual. Like visually, I can envision myself there. Why? Because as I walking around, I saw students by the main quad. There's a huge, very long road, an area there for students to congregate and promote their clubs. When I went, I saw different colors. I saw different people. Asians, Latinos, Persians, everything. A mixture of a whole lot. They were all talking to each other. I thought, "Okay, I want to be here." I say that I want to travel the world and this is a way to travel for me.

I applied to places that I saw people like me. I applied to UC Irvine. I applied there because of the program and because it was really close. Then Cal State Long Beach, I've been there before and it was local. It was really just because of the location.

When it came time to apply, I was around positive peer pressure. Seriously, the Transfer Center changed my academic experience! This is home. The headquarters. John, he was the big brother I never had. That person that knew what I was doing.

He'd get mad because I wasn't being proactive. There was that good peer pressure to say, "You can do it on your own. Even if I wasn't here. You could do it." Building the family here. Building the academic family that I wish I had at home coming from my family, but thankfully I got it here.

When it came time to apply, I was around positive peer pressure. Seriously, the Transfer Center changed my academic experience! This is home. The headquarters. John, he was the big brother I never had. That person that knew what I was doing. He'd get mad because I wasn't being proactive.

Everybody in my social group pressured me to apply to transfer. The Latina Leadership Network. Everybody was like, "Oh, are you applying?" Then if I didn't know about something, I found out through them. The support systems made the difference!

Thankfully, I was admitted to my first and second choice schools, UCLA and UC Irvine. The determining factor, UCLA, was the fact that they had a huge support system for AB540 students like me. I thankfully was able to find role models and mentors through the programs that I had written down from my meeting with Casey. All the stuff that was written on that little piece of paper. I kept that paper with me the whole time.

The determining factor, UCLA, was the fact that they had a huge support system for AB540 students like me.

The reason I went to UCLA was because I had already done the SITE program which is the transfer student program the year before. I lived on campus there. To be honest with you, before that program, I thought, "Okay, maybe I can work towards it." Being there with that program allowed me to feel like a student. I slept in the dorms. I got the UCLA card, the Bruin Card. I went to lectures. I did homework. It was a week to make us feel like we did belong there.

After that, it literally changed my life because school wasn't a priority before that. In my mind I thought, "I need to work to go to school." When I went there, I met people like myself. I felt accepted. I felt liberated from denying who I really, truly was. I embraced the insecurities I had. I made a decision when I came back to follow up on the choices that I had made. Going to that program. Then getting accepted to the scholars program, a mentorship program, I got to have a mentor, a person that I can call and be like, "Oh my gosh! I'm freaking out about this, or can we talk about this? I don't know. I'm not too sure." Having that sense of belonging. It was belonging because I knew I wasn't alone in my fight against the world. That's how you feel. The struggle against the impossible whatever. I met people that were not in my struggle but understood me and empathized with me. That helped me. When I came back I thought, "I can do this." And that's when I decided to leave work and focus on getting out of community college.

Having that sense of belonging. It was belonging because
I knew I wasn't alone in my fight against the world.
That's how you feel.
The struggle against the impossible whatever.
I met people that were not in my struggle but understood me
and empathized with me. That helped me.

Completing the transfer process made me feel like I was walking forward. Made me feel like my life was progressing.

I feel confident that regardless of what happens, I will achieve my goal. I was super, super low at that point when the counselor told me I could not go to a UC because I had a W. I thought I was the worst student ever. I was a low life. I wasn't going to get anywhere. If I can get myself out of that one! I got myself into UCLA! You know what I mean?

A key to my success was the people in the Transfer Center. I promise! Especially after the office got relocated over here cause it was right there in the middle of campus. I would walk to the cafeteria, to have lunch with my friend. Then we would walk by and see the signs about the workshops. Really just being here, physically being here and that sense of support. That family. That connection. Being cared about not only as a student but as a person. The people who work here open their hearts to us. I say 'us' because there's a ton of us that come in.

There are people that can connect to my story. Vince can connect to my story. John can connect to my story. Everybody who works in the Transfer Center! Seriously, I would've probably been lost another few more semesters. Thankfully, it got relocated to a more accessible location for students. Before it was in a hidden location. Because it was more visible to the students, it felt more accessible. So, location made a difference. Because I remember visiting it one time when it was over there. Now in this better location, there is that sense of belonging. Especially being around people from prestigious universities like UC Berkeley. The place is for the rest of us, our crew. The people here are on our team. That's right! It is where everyone belongs.

Really just being here, physically being here
and that sense of support. That family. That connection.
Being cared about not only as a student but as a person.
The people who work here open their hearts to us. I say 'us'
because there's a ton of us that come in.

To be a successful student, you need to be persistent. You have to be willing to ask for help. You have to have courage. Be courageous. You cannot be afraid to fail. Especially at the community college. I don't know the statistics but from my personal experience, my regular classes, I saw a lot of lost folks. Especially in the community college system. Definitely you have to go through those failures to feel successful.

Looking back, I would have not taken that first counselor's feedback so personal. Now I know I should've gone to somebody else. I should've been like, "Well, he's telling me no. Let me go to somebody else." I should have been more active. Back then, I should have been like, "Okay, I'm completely lost." Be honest with people that are trying to help you. "I'm lost, this is my situation."

Students need to be honest with ourselves. Lay it on the table so that they can help you sort it out. Also too, I would've picked a major sooner. Also, I would've looked at schools sooner, too. Be more proactive. Proactive.

I would tell other Latinas to keep going. Continue running. Don't stop!

Profile update: Thalia transferred to the University of California, Los Angeles and graduated with her Bachelor of Arts Degree in Anthropology.

Glossary of Terms

AB540. State of California Assembly Bill 540 is legislation for undocumented immigrants to receive exemption from paying nonresident tuition with provisions under California's Education Code.

A-G Requirements. High school course requirements necessary for admission to the UC and CSU system as first-time freshman.

AP. Advanced Placement courses are designated classes that can count for college credit based on completion of the College Board exam with a qualifying score (usually 3 or higher).

Application fee waiver. A waiver of the application fee awarded by a college based on eligibility criteria. The UC waiver allows the student to apply to four campuses free of charge.

Associate of Arts/Science Degree. The AA/AS Degree includes general education, major, and elective units totaling a minimum of 60 units based on a semester term.

Bachelor of Arts/Science Degree. The BA/BS Degree includes general education, major, and elective units totaling a minimum of 120 units based on a semester term.

Career Center. A student services resource center with information about career planning.

Career/Life Planning Class. A counseling class that discusses steps to finding, exploring, analyzing, and understanding various academic majors, careers, and/or personal interests.

Career/Life Planning Center. Another name for the Career Center. See details above.

Community College. A public open admission post-secondary institution that confers the Associate's Degree and Certificates. There are 113 California community colleges.

CSU's. The California State University System is comprised of 23 campuses. It is the comprehensive public university system of the state of California. I.e. San Diego State, Cal State Fullerton, Cal Poly Pomona, San Francisco State.

EOPS. Extended Opportunity Programs and Services is a state-funded program that provides services above and beyond other student services programs to support low income and underrepresented students in community college. i.e. Book grants, progress reports, early registration, school supplies, testing booklets, etc.

FAFSA. Free Application for Federal Student Aid is a government application required for students to qualify for financial aid distributed by an educational institution.

General Education. A list of college-level courses in subject areas such as Critical Thinking, Arts, Humanities, Computation, Physical Science, Natural Science, English, Foreign Language, etc. taken in addition to prescribed major courses necessary to earn a college degree.

Hispanic. A person whose primary language is Spanish or a person with heritage from a country where the primary language is Spanish.

Honors Program. A program that offers a selection of courses that have been enhanced to provide academic enrichment and support for high achieving students. Students must meet eligibility requirements.

IGETC (Intersegmental General Education Transfer Curriculum). A list of courses articulated with the University of California and California State University systems that meet the necessary lower division general education coursework required to pursue a bachelor's degree.

Latina. A female person residing in the United States whose family's heritage is based in Latin American and/or South American counties.

Latina Leadership Network. A student-run organization (club) that focuses on empowerment and educational attainment of female students with heritage from Latin and South American countries at California community colleges.

MEChA. A student-run organization (club) that focuses on the empowerment and educational attainment of people with ancestral roots in the Southwest United States and Northern Mexico.

Office of Special Programs. A grant-funded resource center with information about various programs at the community college i.e. Honor's Programs, Service Learning, Teacher Preparation, etc.

Puente. A state-funded academic preparation program designed to increase the college-going rate of students from underrepresented demographics with a primary focus on Latino students.

Statement of Intent to Register (SIR). A statement submitted by the student to demonstrate acceptance of the initial offer of admission. A deposit is due at the time of submission.

Transfer. The process of changing enrollment from one institution of higher education to another.

Transfer Center. A student services resource center with information about the transfer process.

UC's. The University of California system is comprised of 9 undergraduate campuses and one graduate campus. It is the premiere, research public university system of the state of California with the flagship campus in the city of Berkeley. I.e. UCLA, UC Irvine, UC San Diego.

Undocumented immigrant. A person residing in the United States with no formal documentation to verify immigration status.

USC. University of Southern California is a private university in California with its main campus located in the city of Los Angeles.

About the Author

Lily E. Espinoza, was born and raised in Fullerton, California. She is a Latina transfer student and an instructor in the Upward Bound program at Mills College in Oakland, California. She has been a professional in higher education since 2001, working with students in middle school, high school, undergraduate and graduate programs. She co-wrote an article in 2012, *Risk and Retention: Are LGBTQ students staying in your community college,* Community College Journal of Research and Practice and developed curriculum for a community college counseling course entitled, *Ensuring Transfer Completion.* She is also the producer and presenter on topics related to college choice on the YouTube channel, *Lily College Mythbusters.* Lily is a single mother to her 13 year old son, Justice. Together they live in the San Francisco Bay Area along with their dog, Max.

ABOOKS

ALIVE Book Publishing and ALIVE Publishing Group
are imprints of Advanced Publishing LLC,
3200 A Danville Blvd., Suite 204, Alamo, California 94507

Telephone: 925.837.7303 Fax: 925.837.6951
www.alivebookpublishing.com

formation can be obtained
Gtesting.com
ne USA
059100718
LV00001B/75/P

CPSIA in
at www.IC
Printed in
LVHW08s
583247